MOTORCYCLE THERAPY

A Canadian Adventure in Central America

by
Jeremy Kroeker

TRAFFORD
PUBLISHING™

Note for Librarians: A cataloguing record for this book is available from Library and Archives
Canada at www.collectionscanada.ca/amicus/index-e.html
ISBN 1-4120-7832-6

Printed in Victoria, BC, Canada. Printed on paper with minimum 30% recycled fibre.
Trafford's print shop runs on "green energy" from solar, wind and other environmentally-friendly power sources.

PUBLISHING™
Offices in Canada, USA, Ireland and UK

Book sales for North America and international:
Trafford Publishing, 6E–2333 Government St.,
Victoria, BC V8T 4P4 CANADA
phone 250 383 6864 (toll-free 1 888 232 4444)
fax 250 383 6804; email to orders@trafford.com
Book sales in Europe:
Trafford Publishing (UK) Limited, 9 Park End Street, 2nd Floor
Oxford, UK OX1 1HH UNITED KINGDOM
phone +44 (0)1865 722 113 (local rate 0845 230 9601)
facsimile +44 (0)1865 722 868; info.uk@trafford.com
Order online at:
trafford.com/05-2730

10 9 8 7 6 5 4 3

For Grandma Helen Kroeker, who understood me.
And for the rest of my family, who never understand but love me
anyway.

"Well, I want to go to South America."
"Listen, Robert, going to another country doesn't make any difference. I've tried all that. You can't get away from yourself by moving from one place to another. There's nothing to that."

- *The Sun Also Rises,* Ernest Hemingway

Introduction

In essence, this is the story of friendship, discovery and reconciliation. Well, that, and what follows when a depressed man spends an entire winter watching the *National Geographic* Channel.

Looking back, I can't tell you how I envisioned that a motorcycle trip from Canmore, Alberta (an hour west of Calgary) to Central or South America would solve my problems. Maybe I hoped to break the inertia my life had developed, to let adventure breathe vitality into a heart that no longer really cared. Maybe that's what I wanted. But that's not what I got. I got something far more valuable... and unsettling. Of course, I didn't know any of this at the time. I only knew one thing.

I needed to ride.

Like every manly adventure (especially ones involving motorcycles, poor planning and high risk of personal injury), this one started with a girl. To thinly disguise her identity, I've changed her name to Susan. I wanted to call her Sauron, after the dark lord from Tolkien's *Lord of the Rings*, but some mutual friends suggested that might be overstating things a bit.

Susan spent an entire year trying to coax me into saying "I love you" for the first time in my life, and I finally did. I meant it, too. She never actually shouted "SUCKER!" at me as she drove off with another guy shortly thereafter, but it was implied.

If the best year of my life began when I kissed her for the first time, then the worst year of my life began when I kissed her goodbye.

But it wasn't all her fault. I had recently quit my job and moved to Canmore for the ice climbing season, an activity that provided solace for me following the difficult breakup. However, within weeks of moving, I sustained an ankle injury while hiking that put me on the couch for the rest of the winter. Suddenly, I had a sturdy tripod of injury, boredom and loneliness on which to display the hollow shell of my heart.

From my living room window, I watched the snowline move down the mountains and retreat again in the spring. Ice climbs formed, ripened and vanished as I huddled before the cold, blue glow of my television.

By early summer, my "tripod of misery" – like the ice – began to crack and falter. My ankle would soon heal and I suppressed boredom by getting a job.

My loneliness, however, proved stubborn and adaptive. It evolved from a sharp pain to a dull ache that at once filled me and pressed against me, making every breath I drew an act of volition. Loneliness fed on my inertia and grew stronger as the summer dragged on. But if I had learned anything from watching ninja movies all winter, I had learned this: a successful warrior uses his opponent's strength to defeat him.

With loneliness comes a certain freedom. Freedom enables mobility and independence. There. I had a new tripod. And what embodies these three elements better than a motorcycle? I formulated a simple, ambiguous plan – to ride south and live happily ever after.

What the plan lacked in specifics I made up for with enthusiasm, rushing out to find a motorcycle just two months prior to my proposed departure. I bought a used 2001 Kawasaki KLR 650, chosen on the merits of its large capacity fuel tank, cost efficiency and simplicity of design. The bike operates on technology developed in the 1980s, which makes it easy to repair with a hammer and duct tape in the rare event of mechanical failure. This particular machine had 9,000 kilometres on the odometer and had already taken its former owner into the wilds of Alaska. In other words, it had far more experience than I did.

Now, the KLR is neither handsome nor particularly smooth to ride. The engineers responsible for its design possibly took their cues from a pneumatic jackhammer. It looks like a big green and silver dirt bike and finds itself equally at home on dirt trails and the highway. That is to say, it does everything reasonably well, but nothing particularly well. It is too heavy for off-road use, and too tall and light for highway comfort. Still, for this trip, it was the right machine.

Almost as an afterthought, I decided to find a travel partner. The ideal companion would have Spanish skills, mechanical aptitude and experience with travel and motorcycles. He would be optimistic, easy-going and, with only one month remaining before I set out, extremely impulsive. In short, I needed a yang to balance my yin.

With such highly specific criteria, only three names came to mind. I fired off some e-mails and one man responded. I'd met Trevor Martens ten years back while travelling in Austria and, while I didn't know him all that well, we had kept up sporadic contact over the years. He met most of my criteria, but what made him the perfect and perfectly eager travel partner was this: his girlfriend had just dumped him.

And so, as Trevor frantically juggled obligations at work in Manitoba with shopping for his own motorcycle, I rode from Canmore to my big send-off in Calgary. Several friends gathered in a suburban back alley of the city's northwest to wish me well. Tolerating my nervous laughter, they offered hugs and handshakes while posing for group photos with the brave hero and the imposing motorcycle that glistened in the sun. The machine roared to life with the push of a button and I revved the engine for dramatic effect. Everyone stood back to let me pass in this, my moment of shining glory.

I revved the engine again and waved goodbye. Then I decided to make a quick, last minute adjustment to my gear. Forgetting to lower the kickstand, I hopped off the bike and it crashed onto its side. It took three of us to hoist the heavily laden bike back onto its wheels. The group disbanded in awkward silence as I dug out my toolkit to repair my clutch and shift levers.

So began my journey to Central America.

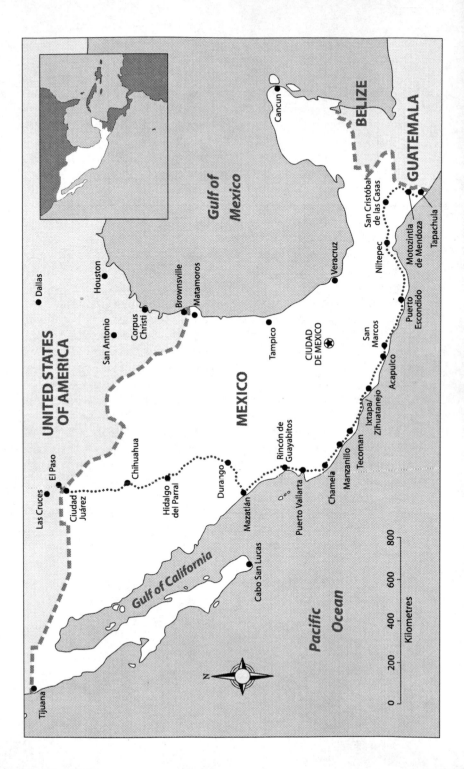

PART

1

October 10

Riding east from Alberta through the Canadian prairies when Central America is clearly south might not make the most geographic sense, but that's what I did – after fixing the bike's clutch and shift levers. Along the way, people often asked me where I was headed. In the grand scheme of things, I had no clear idea. Usually, just to see their reaction, I'd say, "Guatemala." Then I'd strap up my helmet and continue east along the Trans-Canada Highway.

Really, I had two primary destinations in mind. First, since my mom believed that this trip would be my last earthly task, I needed to see her and my dad in Saskatchewan. The visit provided my dad with the opportunity to join me on the trip, at least for a few hours. After I'd said goodbye to my mother, he rode beside me on his 1982 Honda CB750 Custom, finally turning around as I headed farther east to my second destination: Boissevain, Manitoba, to meet Trevor, my companion for the next 14 weeks.

I wore every layer of clothing I had with me, except for my swimming trunks, and I still froze on the ride from Saskatchewan to Trevor's farm. My neck ached from straining against a strong side wind, my knees throbbed with a dull pain, and my eardrums buzzed as if the howl of the wind had become trapped in my head. Fortunately, I knew how to suffer – I was an ice climber. Still, my enthusiasm to ride took a beating and I wondered if I could cope with that level of discomfort on a daily basis. Also, I found myself missing, rather, longing for the girl I'd impulsively begun a relationship with just one month before setting out on the trip. I second-guessed my decision to leave her, but by this time I was fully committed. And, anyway, it was convenient to miss her. It sure beat thinking about Susan.

I pulled into Trevor's driveway and parked beside the mirror image of my bike. Apparently, Trevor had purchased the identical make, model and year of motorcycle so that we could carry fewer parts between us. That's a farmer's logic for you.

I eagerly dismounted my machine, removed my helmet and turned to face the biggest Rottweiler I'd ever seen. The slavering beast eyed me intently from the back of a pickup truck, quietly licking its chops as if in anticipation of a wonderful meal. It's the quiet dogs that worry me.

Before I could actually pass out in fear, the front door of the house blew open and Trevor tumbled outside to greet me with a flurry of playful punches and smart-ass comments. Meanwhile, the dog leapt from the truck, tripping over itself with enthusiasm, and nearly bowled me over by affectionately leaning its full weight against my thighs.

"You remember Daisy?" asked Trevor. "She looks mean, but she's a big suck."

Trevor looked just as I remembered him from years ago, except that his straight blond hair had been trimmed to fit neatly under his dirty baseball cap. He was tall and lanky, but strong. Thick eyebrows guarded dark, sunken eyes – giving him a simian appearance when he was confused, and an intense, serious look at most other times. A strong jaw provided the anchor for his facial features, tipping the scales decidedly towards the description "ruggedly handsome."

As for me, my wavy brown hair was pressed against my head from wearing a helmet all day and hung like a curtain in front of my blue eyes and broad nose. Normally, literary license might allow me to use the

word "handsome" in my own description, but at that moment "dishev-
elled" fit much better.

Trevor and I went inside and talked excitedly late into the night about
old times and new adventures.

October 18

We spent a few days at Trevor's farm gazing out of his kitchen window
into thick, cold fog and making some last-minute preparations. Trevor
overhauled his carburetor, installed a new drive chain and sprockets,
welded a luggage rack for his bike and created some highway pegs for
my machine while I stood around, alternately poking Trevor and my
motorbike with my index finger. I played with Daisy a bit, too.

When it came time to inventory our tools and spare parts, Trevor
noticed that I had purchased the wrong drive chain in Calgary. Trevor's
mom agreed to mail it back to the dealer for a refund, but we'd have to
buy another chain somewhere along the way.

Eventually the fog lifted. Trevor and I bundled ourselves against the
elements with an impressive collection of winter apparel, none of which
was designed for motorcycle riding (with the exception of Trevor's outer
jacket). Trevor's parents filmed our awkward departure as we rolled along
the farm's gravel driveway. We turned left onto the highway, pointing
our machines south and accelerating hard towards the sun.

The very next day I wore jeans and a T-shirt on the ride through
South Dakota, and for the first time in my life I didn't wear a helmet.
The wind sucked the moisture from my eyes and pinned my hair back,
exposing my pale forehead to the sun like an egg in an incubator. I fail to
understand the affinity dogs have for sticking their heads out of moving
vehicles. To alleviate discomfort, I wore a bandanna on my head and
another one over my face, effectively destroying the cool biker image
Peter Fonda had established in *Easy Rider*.

Trevor and I rode side by side. As I looked over to give him a big
"thumbs-up," the wind ripped the sunglasses from my face. The glasses
fluttered through the air, landing perfectly in the wheel rut of an
approaching vehicle, which swerved to miss them. I put my helmet
back on at the next stop.

Apart from that, we basically travelled 600 uneventful kilometres down Highway 83, the longest highway in North America (according to a greasy placemat that I saw in a roadside diner). We rode into the night and pitched our tent in a grass field behind a little truck stop north of Pierre, South Dakota.

The atmosphere of giddy excitement and high adventure within the nylon walls of Trevor's tent reminded me of my first campout as a little boy in my parents' back yard. Trevor and I lay in our sleeping bags, comparing notes about our first day, finally laughing ourselves to sleep when we discovered that we had each been honking at every animal and most people that we'd passed since leaving home.

October 19

I'll wager that even Lewis and Clark had difficulty thinking of something to say about Nebraska and Kansas. We rolled past a looping backdrop of corn, farms and pheasants. At least the monotony gave us a chance to think about our heading.

To escape the wrath of winter, Trevor and I had ridden south as directly as possible. Suddenly, we faced our first specific decision. I wanted to rip through Mexico along the east coast, and Trevor wanted to leisurely explore the west. Following a short debate, we decided to ride west. After spending the night in Liberal, Kansas in a cheap hotel, we left southbound Highway 83. Highway 54 angled southwest through the semi-arid, undulating grassland of the Oklahoma panhandle, cut through the vast expanse of northwestern Texas, and delivered us finally to Santa Rosa, New Mexico.

One more day of riding in sweltering heat brought us back to Texas and into the concrete jungle of El Paso, perched on the US-Mexican border.

October 21

Trevor and I had left Canada with enough spare parts to build a motorcycle from scratch. Unfortunately, the bike would have been remarkably dissimilar to the ones we had.

You make certain assumptions when you buy parts from a dealer.

Never mind that the monkey behind the counter is some high school punk working weekends so he can get discounts on body armour. When you ask for a chain and oil filter for a 2001 Kawasaki KLR 650, you don't expect to receive a chain and oil filter for a 1967 Harley Davidson. You just take your merchandise, fork over billions of dollars, and walk away feeling like you've been violated, but at least confident that you have the correct parts.

Of course, this confidence is completely unwarranted. The kid does not care that the success of your trip across Central America, and perhaps your personal safety, depends on having the right equipment to repair your machine. He cares about the girl in the showroom trying on seat-less leather chaps.

Suffice it to say, the chain and oil filters I bought in Canada were incorrect. We had caught the problem with the chain in Canada, but we only noticed that I had the wrong filters now because Trevor needed to buy some spares. When I pulled out my filters to check the part number, it became evident that they would not fit my engine.

We found a large bike shop in El Paso called Edge Motorsports, and purchased the chain. Still, they didn't stock the oil filters we needed, nor did any other bike shop in the city.

Furthermore, Trevor needed to find protective guards for his brake and shift levers. He made several phone calls and forays into the city to look for the guards to no avail before an Edge employee offered to sell Trevor the guards from his personal bike.

We followed Javier to his house when he got off work, after receiving best wishes and two shirts emblazoned with the Edge Motorsports logo from the shop owners. We worked late into the night at Javier's place, switching the bark busters from one bike to another. Well, Trevor and Javier worked late; I held the flashlight and drank 7-Up.

October 22

Our entire trip budget consisted of a meagre 4,000 Canadian dollars, and every day we spent in the States eroded our financial resources. Feeling rushed by our limited funds, and yet ill-prepared to enter Mexico, we paid for another night at the motel in El Paso, adding to our stress.

Perhaps it was for the best. While riding to Javier's place, I noticed that my drive chain had become increasingly noisy and in constant need of adjustment. I knew that I'd have to replace it at some point on the trip, but I had no idea it would be so soon.

Whenever you replace the chain on a bike, you should also replace both sprockets, but I figured I could do that before lunch and then hang out at the mall. I tend to be uncharacteristically optimistic about my ability to perform mechanical repairs.

I parked my bike on the shady side of the hotel parking lot for the project. Stuffing my backpack under the bike's frame to elevate the rear wheel, I removed the wheel and sprocket, sawed through the riveted chain with a hacksaw, and fought for nearly an hour to install the new chain as the blazing sun eroded my precious shade.

I worked alone while Trevor laboured on the phone. He needed to find a chiropractor to take the edge off his back pain – pain that had become more acute since our trip had begun. Between phone calls to various chiropractors, he placed several calls to bike shops in an effort to locate our elusive oil filters.

Occasionally I'd drop my tools and sprint up the stairs to our room in a sweaty panic, barraging Trevor with questions in a greasy, wide-eyed frenzy of mechanical ignorance. He patiently answered my questions, effectively walking me through the extremely simple job.

Before rushing off to his chiropractor appointment, Trevor arranged for a bike dealer in Las Cruces, New Mexico to ship some oil filters to us. We rode to the bus depot in the evening to see if they had arrived. They had, but they were the same wrong filters that I'd bought in Calgary. Apparently, the Kawasaki parts website contained an error (all apologies to teenaged parts department monkeys).

Trevor quickly called the shop in Las Cruces and caught the parts manager in the process of locking up for night. After explaining our predicament, we shipped the wrong filters back COD and had another four sent to us. The correct filters arrived late at night. We had been on the road for four days, stuck and under stress for two more, and we hadn't even entered Mexico yet.

October 23

While Trevor frantically packed and repacked his gear, I reviewed the border checklist in my head. I had the requisite paperwork and copies of every document. I'd memorized a few Spanish phrases: "Please don't shoot me" and "We're not travelling together." I felt prepared for the worst.

After half an hour of navigation along labyrinthine super highways that streaked through the sky, we killed our engines and coasted up to the border. I removed my helmet, careful not to make any sudden movements. The guard looked genuinely annoyed as he motioned for me to keep moving. Just like that, we found ourselves in the chaos of Juarez —breathing Mexican exhaust, covered in Mexican dust, and dodging Mexican traffic.

Diesel smoke burned my eyes as I searched for signs to lead us out of the city along Highway 45. Failing to find any, we navigated by instinct and soon found the open road heading south through sandy plains of sage brush and dry grass. I thought of the frigid beauty of the Canadian Rockies and marvelled that it had taken just a week of riding to enter a country so vastly different from mine.

For 30 kilometres we paralleled a barbed-wire fence with closely spaced, twisted fence posts fashioned from thorny branches before encountering the *real* border. We parked the bikes, gathered our papers and went inside to deal with customs. It only took us an hour to get our visas and temporary import permits.

"Well, we're in Mexico," said Trevor.

"And we rode here," I added with a little pride.

We arrived in Chihuahua as the sun kissed the horizon, desperate to find sanctuary before dark. In our frantic search we stopped at the first motel we saw on the edge of town.

The proprietor approached us before we could dismount our bikes. Two women followed: the younger, more attractive woman clutched the arm of the other with a defensive but curious look about her. Her eyes locked onto me as the strange trio approached.

I removed my helmet to address the male manager.

"How much?" I asked in Spanish.

"140 pesos," he replied, "for six hours."

I looked at Trevor. It sounded like he'd said 140 pesos for six hours. Now, why would we pay for six hours? That would only give us until midnight.

"How much for the entire night?" I persisted.

"That's not possible," the manager said. "Only six hours."

Of course, to the streetwise traveller, it would have been apparent what sort of motel this was. Even the name suggested what we, two naïve boys from the Canadian prairies, were slowly beginning to understand: the Mirage Motel, with its flashing pink and blue neon sign and private parking stalls, was a den of the sexually damned. That explained the salacious stare of the moderately attractive girl, who now stood uncomfortably close to me, and why she kept getting closer.

We felt our innocence ebbing away with every moment and opted for a hasty retreat, but my bike wouldn't start. Like zombies from a bad movie, the unholy trio crept closer and closer as I tried to engage the engine. Trevor had to give me a push to start the bike and we fatalistically sped into the black heart of the city to meet certain peril.

The streets became darker, busier, and our stress levels began to spike. Then Trevor spotted a low-budget hotel. He guarded the bikes while I inspected the room, but realistically, as long as I found no dead hookers on the floor, it would do just fine. The manager let us wheel our bikes inside the hotel for the night.

While Trevor showered, I fixed the problem with my starter. It must have been a simple loose connection because, just when I had exhausted my mechanical resourcefulness by jiggling a bunch of wires, the problem disappeared.

October 24

The day began with a quick stop at a tourist office. The bubble-headed tourist representative gave us obsolete maps and instructed us to ride many kilometres against opposing traffic on a one-way street. When we discovered the subtle flaw in her directions we pulled over to scour our maps for an alternative route, quickly discovering that her plan, though highly dangerous and illegal, certainly smacked of efficiency. We took her advice, much to the dismay of local motorists.

Breaking free of the city, we followed a smooth black road that shimmered in the dry heat from Chihuahua to Hidalgo del Parral. Red stone walls slashed through a landscape of buttes and conical hills with the linear precision of surgical incisions, delineating one pasture from another. Short, billowy trees, like balls of green cotton, and the occasional patch of pink wildflowers lent colour to the otherwise brown grassland.

The ride marked the first time in my life I have ever altered the course of a motor vehicle to avoid a spider. As black as the road, the spider initially appeared to be a lump of asphalt or a shoe belonging to a small child. I narrowly avoided it and watched in my mirror as Trevor approached. When he suddenly noticed the tarantula out of the corner of his eye, his foot shot up like he needed to scratch his ear with it and he veered to avoid the beast. The tarantula never moved.

October 25

Little family-operated stores, or *tiendas*, splattered with Coca-Cola or Pepsi posters, dot the roadside. The single-storey shacks are typically constructed from bricks and plaster, and capped with corrugated steel roofs. Some of the fancier *tiendas* have an actual service window with a heavy wooden shutter that swings down from above when closed, but most simply have a door and one or two square holes in the wall that pass for windows. The *tiendas* offer little in the way of convenience, but giving a dollar to a struggling family appealed to us more than spending 75 cents at a modern service station.

The tienda that we stopped at for a break was part of a simple three-room home. It had a table with white plastic chairs, a small kitchen, and a colour TV hooked up to an Xbox. The middle-aged shopkeeper welcomed us into her home and sold us drinks out of the fridge. Her two little boys shifted their gaze from us to our bikes.

"Why aren't you in school?" I asked.

"It's Saturday," said the oldest boy.

"I see."

The boys got excited when we started our engines. We waved to them and rode off. When I checked my mirrors, I noticed the boys running after us on the highway.

October 26

I heard Trevor rushing to the bathroom several times during the night. Just before our alarm sounded he informed me he felt too sick to ride, and I breathed a quiet sigh of relief; I could hear the patter of rain on the roof of the hotel and I didn't relish the thought of getting up before the sun.

Trevor stayed in our windowless hotel room in Durango to wrestle with the Angel of Death, while I lounged in the nearly vacant foyer and cast seductive glances at the cute girl at the front desk. Of course, this strategy for picking up girls has never, ever succeeded in the history of inter-gender relationships, especially where a language barrier is involved. Although, I hoped the language barrier would work in my favour; I tend to make irreparably poor impressions on women because my brain and mouth work independently.

The girl, Cynthia, motioned to me and told me I had a phone call. I expected it was Trevor, though I couldn't remember seeing a phone in our room. I put my book down and swaggered over to the desk, taking the phone from Cynthia with a wink.

"Hello?"

"Who are you?" blurted the guy on the other end in an American accent. He proceeded to bombard me with questions, some of which became fairly personal.

"Who are YOU?" I demanded.

"Gus. I'm a friend of Cynthia's."

Ah, the poor girl, I thought. She must have fallen prey to my staring and swaggering and enlisted her English-speaking friend to quiz me. Sometimes I forget the overwhelming nature of my sexual appeal and I use it irresponsibly.

For some reason, Gus desperately wanted to show me an Internet café and appeared at the door within seconds of hanging up the phone. He wore a white T-shirt and tight, beige pants designed to be baggy. A tangle of black hair covered Gus's bulky head, a head that attached to his slumped shoulders without proper segue.

He removed the headset for his tape player as he shuffled his ample frame in Cynthia's direction. After greeting her and saying something outrageously funny in Spanish, he slowly turned to me and introduced himself. Gus was an American, no surprise there, who aspired to produce, direct and star in an Internet soap opera. The details were sketchy, but, from what I gathered, the show would clearly defy international law and be an affront to human dignity.

Still sick, but eager to get out of the hotel after a hard day of vomiting, Trevor dragged himself down to the lobby and the three of us headed out onto the darkened street.

"So, are you guys fans of Rod Stewart?" Gus asked.

We laughed, and then realised he wasn't kidding.

"No? What about his song *Broken Arrow?*" he said.

"Uh, I've never... I don't know."

"Man, I love that song."

To prove it, Gus put his headphones on and played *Broken Arrow* loud enough for us to hear. He seemed particularly fond of part of the song. He played 30 seconds, and then rewound the tape and listened to the same 30 seconds over and over and over.

"This guy's nuts," whispered Trevor during a short musical interlude. Gus turned the music down when we arrived at the café. I should mention that the word "café" gets horribly abused in Mexico. We entered a smoky room containing a ceiling fan, half a dozen off-white computers and some dirty plastic chairs. While I checked my e-mail, Gus sat beside me, surfing porn and trying to get me to sign up as a women's prison pen pal.

"These women are lonely!" he insisted. Then he stared at me... intently... for a really long time.

By then I understood that Cynthia had not tried to glean information about me by recruiting Gus; she had paired up two of her most undesirable admirers for the evening, temporarily removing them from her sphere of consciousness, the little vixen. Leaving the café, we declined Gus's invitation to view his apartment (I could already see it in my mind's eye). We said goodbye to Gus and watched him plod into the night to the faint sound of Rod Stewart's *Broken Arrow.*

October 28

The serpentine road between Durango and Mazatlan bears the name *el Espinazo Del Diablo* – the Devil's Spine. Terrible beauty overshadows the hazards of the road as it carves through the Sierra Madre Occidental Mountains, tempting motorists to follow its precipitous path and leading many of them to crumpled metal graves.

An ominous fog enshrouded the Devil's Spine as we left Durango. The cold penetrated every layer of warm clothing, and my fingers tingled with pain. It was both a relief and a revelation when the clouds began to lift and we could see farther than 50 metres in front of us, down into the valleys.

The bank dropped steeply away on one side and rose sharply into towering columns of volcanic rock on the other. Elaborate memorial shrines dotted the narrow shoulders. One particularly deadly corner, its banks proving too steep for any recovery effort, displayed dozens of crosses and the twisted shells of vehicles that had plunged over its side... graphic reminders of the frailty of life.

The sound of our engines rising and falling to negotiate sharp curves and steep hills added fuel to the flame of exhilaration within. Wind whistled off my helmet and snapped at my blue nylon jacket. Perhaps, more than anything, it's the *sound* of riding a motorbike that makes you feel alive and transforms every man into a boy.

As I approached a sharp hairpin turn, I could see Trevor below, riding in the opposite direction. It was a perfect moment. I became acutely aware that this snapshot in time would remain in my mind forever. At that moment, there was nothing else I would rather have been doing anywhere on earth. It took me 30 years to learn this, but perfect moments happen more than we realize. The trick is to recognize them when they appear and really live in them. You can ruin a perfect moment by worrying about the past or the future. Perfect moments fade – there will always be time to worry when they are gone.

Shortly after that, we pulled off the road for a break. The temperature had warmed up enough that I regained proper use of my fingers, and I removed an outer layer of clothing. I drank some water, had a snack, jumped back on my bike and started the engine. I wanted to reach Mazatlan in daylight, so we could relax before bed. I looked over at Trevor. He continued to fumble with gear in search of his water bottle.

I killed my engine.

It never failed: by the time I wanted to leave, Trevor had only just started to eat. He didn't mean to be slow. It's just that he seemed to pack his most frequently used items (like water) beneath a mountain of infrequently used gear (like the tent). And he still didn't have a system. He routinely rearranged the configuration of his gear so that he could never quite remember the location of anything.

I glanced at my watch and back at Trevor, now frantically stuffing things back into his pack. I felt a hot rush of blood to my head as I thought about the descending arc of the sun and how far we still had to ride. I no longer wondered if we would have time to relax before dark; I wondered if we would even make our destination.

Trevor finally got back on his bike and we took off. We rode a whole 15 kilometres before he signalled me to pull over. He couldn't find his wallet. I watched him unpack his bike yet again. Following a long, unsuccessful search, Trevor rode back to our rest spot while I waited. I would have accompanied him, but we had a short supply of fuel and we couldn't afford for both of us to run out of gas.

I paced the gravel lot of a small brick hut plastered with Pepsi posters, telling myself that I could easily have made the same mistake, and to let it go. The truth is, my reaction to Trevor's inefficiency underscored a flaw in my character and I wasn't proud of it. I saw my impatience as an emotional response, one that I could identify but not control. I've heard that if you act calm, you'll be calm. Well, at the best of times I can act patient, I just don't know if I can *be* patient.

A few children stared at me from the doorway of their hut. I waved at them and they scurried out of sight.

After half an hour I heard Trevor's engine. I could tell that he'd found the wallet by the way he rode up to me, shouting happily through his closed visor. In his excitement he skidded to a stop, neglected the kickstand and dropped the bike on the parking lot. Trevor's relief at finding his wallet outweighed the embarrassment of the crash, and the entertainment value of the incident outweighed my frustration. Before helping Trevor lift his fallen machine, I dug out my camera and snapped a picture of him standing over it in comic shame.

It felt great to get back on the bike. The road descended through thick trees to a valley floor, where it disappeared beneath running water. A three-foot waterfall distinctly defined the left side of the road, but no handy landscape feature indicated where the right side ended.

We watched a large truck roll through. The water looked shallow, maybe two feet in depth. Trevor crossed first so he could get a photo of me, and signalled when he had prepared the shot.

I started across. Normally I'd scan the roadway for potholes and obstacles, but the muddy water made that impossible. Riding through while watching flowing water tends to make you drift in its direction, in this case from right to left towards a waterfall, so I fixed my gaze on the far bank to where the road emerged. I kept to the middle in case I suddenly hit something underwater that might knock me off course. Once safely on the other side, I turned around and made the crossing again, mostly for fun, but also so Trevor could get a picture with my camera, too.

We continued and crossed the Tropic of Cancer, an imaginary line that parallels the equator and marks the point where the sun is directly overhead at noon on the summer solstice. The line seemed magical because, as soon as we crossed it, the temperature jumped several degrees and the air became noticeably humid. Trevor said he could smell the ocean.

Despite the magic, Trevor and I had our first real argument that night at the hotel in Mazatlan. I expressed frustration over our slow pace, and he expressed frustration with our fast pace. Then we talked about money: after a few calculations, we quickly realized that we had already spent nearly 20 percent of our budget… 20 percent! That meant, on average, it was costing us one dollar for every five kilometres we traveled. As we still lacked a specific destination, we didn't know how concerned we should be about that – but if our money continued to dwindle at the established rate we would run out of cash before leaving Mexico. That, we could not accept.

October 29

With nearly 5,000 additional kilometres since its last service in Manitoba, my bike needed an oil change. On the way out of town, I bought oil at a dealer that charged per litre what OPEC charges per barrel. Unfortunately, regular oil changes are not optional.

Almost immediately, we found ourselves on a four-lane toll road. Trevor and I had intended to avoid toll roads for two reasons. First, the free roads, narrow and winding, offered a more authentic Mexican experience. Second, we had no money for tolls. We tried to escape from the toll-way, but they design those things like lobster traps. To get back onto the free highway, we each had to surrender 32 pesos.

Around noon, we stopped at a little town and pushed our bikes beside a transport truck, desperately squeezing into a thin strip of shade by pressing up against the canvas-covered trailer. Before we could even take off our helmets, three little boys gathered around our machines.

"Where are you from?" they asked.

"Canada."

The boys' eyes grew wide. They stared at us and each other as if we'd said Mars.

"Is it cold in Canada?"

"Yes. Very cold. That's why we're here."

"Here it is always hot," they said.

"I know. I'm hot right now. I'm always hot."

The boys gave each other strange looks and started laughing and pushing each other. In retrospect, that provided the first indication that my Spanish was seriously flawed. Later (much later, I'm afraid), I learned that every time I meant to say "I am hot," I actually said "I am horny." I told nearly everyone from Texas to Guatemala that I was horny, which explains why most conversations ended abruptly when the subject turned to weather.

Eventually, the driver of our shady refuge needed to move the truck. He pointed at our maps and told us about construction on the free road, advising us to take the toll-way. We didn't really understand his instructions. He patiently repeated himself, pointing at the map and using progressively smaller sentences. Finally, he resorted to visual aids, grabbing a handful of the sticky rocks that coated his running boards and dropping them on the ground by our feet. Satisfied that we caught his general meaning – that tar and tiny pebbles covered the free road, making the drive unpleasant, slow, and dangerous for motorbikes – he waved goodbye and drove off with our shade.

We ignored the trucker's sage advice and rode a few kilometres on the tar and pebbles, but the oncoming traffic sprayed us with rocks that stuck to our bikes and clothing. We backtracked and hit the toll-way as the trucker had advised.

After a few short kilometres we left it to follow a road that wound through fields of tall, grassy sugarcane and broad-leaved banana trees, and then into dense forest. The leaves reached out to us from all sides, including the canopy, creating living tunnels through which we caught occasional glimpses of an evening sun sparkling off the Pacific Ocean.

We stopped for the night in the little town of Rincón de Guayabitos, just north of Puerto Vallarta, and unloaded our bikes in the courtyard of a little bungalow near the beach.

After supper we walked to the ocean, through dark, nearly empty streets. We'd just entered a sparsely lit alley when we noticed three men closing in behind us. Neither Trevor nor I is prone to panic or irrational fear. However, we both felt suddenly uneasy and paused under a dim street light at the edge of the dark beach. The men stopped as well, as if waiting for us to leave the light. Trevor and I considered our options. We were probably just being paranoid, but we listened to our instincts and turned around.

We walked back towards the men, who kept their eyes on us as they blocked the alley. I said hello and they parted to let us pass. We found an alternative route to the beach and walked nervously along the dark shore.

October 30

For lunch we pulled in at a restaurant with whitewashed stucco walls and a tile floor, the restaurant brimming with boisterous Mexican men. Wearing white cowboy hats and black moustaches, the men crowded around tables covered with red and white tablecloths, and they all turned to stare at us when we walked in. At least the music never stopped.

It seemed we got this sort of reaction a lot. Apparently, stopping at places that tourists seldom visit and travelling with motorbikes that dwarf most others on Mexican roads makes one a bit of a novelty. People often turned to stare, or pointed at us while whispering to their friends, but they never meant any harm and we got used to it. On this day, the restaurant patrons quickly lost interest in us and we sat down to a cheap meal filled with spices that made a layer of skin slough off my tongue.

We planned to stop in Chamela for the night. According to our maps, Chamela anchored the junction of two major roads and maintained a population large enough to support an airport. Our guidebook suggested that we might find free camping there along one of many private beaches owned by local resort hotels. Accidentally riding past such a major landmark is nearly impossible, but we managed it somehow and found ourselves searching for the next town on our maps, Careytos.

We pulled off the highway to ask directions from some grubby men in front of a cluster of weathered shacks. We killed our engines and removed our helmets. The men, for once, barely noticed.

"Where is Careytos?" I asked.

The men glanced over but continued talking amongst themselves.

"Hey! Where is Careytos?" I asked again.

"There," said one of the men. He pointed to the shacks. Everyone laughed except for me and Trevor.

"We need a place to stay," I interrupted.

"Try Chamela," they suggested.

"Yeah, we already tried that," I said. "It's gone."

The men just shrugged.

Trevor thought he had spotted a sign for a fancy hotel right in the middle of nowhere about a kilometre back, so we turned to check it out. The sign and gate belonged to a guarded, private community for the obnoxiously wealthy. We rode through the gate and up meandering, cobblestone roads that felt slippery and squeaked beneath our tires. One road led us high onto a terrace overlooking the ocean, but at every turn we encountered ornate, iron gates that barred access to private drives.

A white Dodge Durango appeared at intervals on the otherwise desolate streets, as if the driver was monitoring us. Trevor and I stopped to look at our maps and the Durango rolled up beside us. The driver appeared to be in his late forties. He had an athletic build and curly grey hair. When asked if he spoke English he replied, "I would certainly hope so. I'm from South Africa."

He introduced himself as Eeyore, like the donkey. At least, that's what Trevor heard. I thought he said Peyore, which seemed unfortunate. Perhaps our ears were still ringing from the noise of the highway because, when asked to kindly repeat his name, I heard Peyore again, and Trevor heard Eeyore. Consequently, we both mumbled his name or simply trailed off whenever proper etiquette called for its insertion.

Peyore offered to show us a free campsite on a private beach if we didn't mind a quick stop at his house to pick up his dogs. We followed him up the cobblestone road to the very apex of a small mountain. He paused at his own iron gate and asked if we would like to come in for a cold beer while we waited. Trevor accepted eagerly, but I had my reservations. Peyore seemed nice enough, but I couldn't understand why he had been following us earlier or why he, obviously a very wealthy man, would go out of his way to play host to us – two filthy travellers seeking free accommodation.

It just felt odd. Trevor couldn't understand my apprehension and I couldn't give him a reason for it. Then it came to me: the situation reminded me of Christmas Eve in Vienna long ago, when I'd first accepted the hospitality of a stranger. It became the worst travel experience of my life.

It was already late. Soon after my train arrived, the station emptied. People rushed off to be with their family and friends, leaving me, some homeless people and a skeleton staff of janitors beneath the yellow lights in the cold cavern of the Vienna train station.

I hurried to a pay phone in the parking lot. Not one single budget hostel had a vacancy. I hung up the phone and wandered dumbly into the night, sorely alone and feeling sorry for myself.

Then I heard a voice from behind me, addressing me in German.

"I don't speak German," I said in German.

"Ah. Change. Do you have change?" the man said in English.

I really didn't. Then he introduced himself and asked if I needed a place to stay. Peter assured me that his wife and child would gladly have me as their Christmas guest. I'm usually hesitant to accept hospitality, especially from strangers who ask for spare change, but I had no other place to go.

I quickly sized him up. A diminutive, middle-aged man, Peter had wispy brown hair that looked as though it might abandon him at any moment. He wore glasses, a brown overcoat and a pair of plaid dress pants. If it came to physical confrontation, I would prevail. I glanced around the parking lot, then swallowed hard and followed him to his car.

We drove into the strange city, communicating poorly through broken English and German. I kept my pack on my lap and my hand on the door handle.

Before I knew it we had left the city, travelling along a twisty country lane choked with tall, dark hedges. A gentle rain flashed in the headlights against a backdrop of churning fog. I drew quick, shallow breaths and tried to moisten my lips, but my mouth had stopped producing saliva several kilometres back.

Peter seemed pleasant enough and made no threats, but I had a feeling of impending doom. Did he have friends lurking around the corner? Did he have a weapon? I had no control over the situation.

A clock struck midnight when we arrived at Peter's abode. I stopped dead in my tracks upon the threshold and the hair on the back of my neck stood on end. Perhaps the apartment bothered me, or the fact that Peter stood behind me, blocking my escape and breathing rapidly though his nose as if in anticipation.

What had Peter said in the train station? He'd said he had a wife and child who would welcome me for dinner. But my German was poor. Maybe he'd *killed* his wife and child and planned to *eat* them for dinner.

The apartment consisted of one room that reeked of bachelorhood and lonely desperation – not unlike my own apartment in Canada, but that's not the point. It contained a small area for cooking, a black leather couch, and one large bed ringed with pictures of naked women. I quickly scanned the images for naked men and found none, to my small relief.

I shuffled into the apartment and stood aside to let Peter pass, keeping my back against the wall so I could keep my eye on him. The heavy wooden door swung shut and Peter locked it with a key from the inside. The deadbolt slid into place with a heavy *chunk* that reverberated through my head, if not the room.

Pure willpower kept me awake through several hours of Peter's home movies, but eventually I couldn't keep my eyes open any longer. Sensing this, Peter suddenly stripped to a pair of white briefs and bounded across the room to his bed. Pulling the blankets back with a flourish, he hopped into bed, propped himself up on one elbow and patted the mattress, beckoning me hither.

A rather fascinating debate ensued regarding cultural differences, personal space and male bonding. Though Peter certainly made a number of excellent points, the argument swung to my favour when I finally threatened to break the heavy wooden door with Peter's skull if he would not let me leave.

Now standing on the bed in all his tighty-whitey splendour, looking somewhat dejected, Peter offered to drive me back to the train station. I roughly knew the way. If he deviated from the route, I decided that I would leap from his moving car and flee into the night, but it never came to that. I found myself back at the station at three in the morning, my head and limbs buzzing with fatigue.

I needed a place to lie down. Even a cold, hard bench would do... a cold, hard bench, like the one I could see through locked glass doors. Cupping my hands against the glass, I stared at the bench with bloodshot eyes. The gentle rain turned to sleet. As my family gathered for dinner on Christmas Eve back in Canada, I crawled beneath a concrete staircase, put my pack on the wet sidewalk and tried to sleep.

I drifted in and out of consciousness for a while before noticing an unpleasant but familiar smell. I had trouble placing it, until I noticed a man urinating on the sidewalk. The warm, steaming fluid trickled down the concrete to where I lay. I had made a bed of the wet pavement stained by the urine of countless vagrants. At least Jesus had a manger.

So that explained my unease as I faced Peyore, but – as I tried to tell myself now – the situations didn't really compare. After all, Peyore spoke English, I had my own transportation, and I had a friend. Still, I took a long time to make up my mind before finally suppressing my instincts and following Trevor onto Peyore's property.

I'm glad I did – I thought houses like that only existed in movies. The courtyard and infinity pool overlooked the ocean. If you dropped a glass from the stone wall that delineated earth and sky, it would flutter 100 metres through the air before shattering on Peyore's private beach. To reach the sand you had to navigate a steep, winding flight of 204 stairs down the cliff. (There used to be 206 stairs, Peyore told us, but two had been removed to accommodate a beach-front patio.)

A gardener in uniform quietly tended the grounds while we sipped our beer and took in the view. We sat at a thick wooden table on wooden chairs sheltered by a high thatched roof, listening to music from an invisible sound system. So, I suppose we never actually saw Peyore's house, just part of his back yard.

"What do you do?" I exclaimed when I first stepped through the gate.

"Well, we just try to live," said Peyore.

Right. Never ask a wealthy man living in Mexico how he became wealthy. Bad form, Jeremy.

When we finished our beer, Peyore took us to a private beach where we could camp for free. He told the security guard at the gate that we should be allowed to come and go as we pleased, leaving Trevor and me to our own slice of paradise. After pitching our tent, we cooked supper in the sleepy light of a setting sun while listening to the surf break just 200 metres away.

Accepting hospitality from strangers is a risky business. In Austria, it accounted for one of my worst travel experiences, but here in Mexico, it led to one of my best. The two nights sort of cancelled each other out. Balance had been restored to my travel world.

But something else bothered me that night.

The nylon walls of the tent gently billowed as if breathing the warm evening air. I lay in my sleeping bag, watching a thick shadow creep up the white fabric, swallowing the orange glow of the sunset from bottom to top. Soon, the rhythmic sound of the ocean would lull me to sleep as it had already done for Trevor, which brought me to the fly in my ointment.

That night, a spectacular night that will undoubtedly live in my memory forever, had a subtle flaw. It's just that I've seen some of the most romantic places in the world, but always with other guys.

October 31

We had been carefully following signs for Tecoman until the signs suddenly vanished on the outskirts of Manzanillo. It was as if the Department of Highways went, "Well, we've done all we can do. If they can't find Tecoman on their own from here, they never had a chance."

Imagine if this happened in Canada. You're a foreigner travelling from Calgary to Toronto and the last sign as you approach Winnipeg reads, "Toronto 2,400 kilometres." You pass several key, unmarked intersections. The sun goes down.

If you are lucky, you wind up in the Exchange district, where friendly Manitobans will direct you to a local pub. If you are unlucky, you wind up in the "Murder 500 Block," where members of the Manitoba Warriors will instruct you on how to escape with your life. Either way, you're not much closer to Toronto.

Needless to say, Trevor and I guessed incorrectly at countless intersections. When the dust settled, we found ourselves riding in the wrong direction along an expensive toll road – a road that we could not afford to take. The only way to regain the free road without paying a toll would have been to cross a steep concrete ditch, four lanes of busy highway, and drive against the flow of traffic on a busy off-ramp.

Now that I see it in writing, I can't believe we considered it. Anyway, Trevor dismissed the idea because of the "impossible" traverse across the ditch... a traverse that I considered feasible. An intense argument erupted over whether or not we could even make the crossing, an argument that continued long after we'd agreed on the stupidity of the manoeuvre. It was a moot point. When the fight ended, we continued along the toll road.

But I had a moot point to prove. When I saw a break in traffic I rode towards the ditch. Standing on my pegs to lower the bike's centre of gravity, I charged off the road and down the steep gradient like a miniature *Man from Snowy River*. My front suspension compressed violently when I hit bottom. Taking a second to recover, I accelerated hard out of the ditch towards opposing traffic. I rode back through the ditch a bit faster on the return trip, bottoming out the suspension again and flashing Trevor a look that clearly said, "I told you so."

In spite of the heat, an icy silence hung between me and Trevor when we stopped for lunch. I wanted to ask the waitress for a different glass, but I didn't know the right word and Trevor had the Spanish dictionary... which is why I ended up asking her for a different penis.

November 2

Trevor and I split up for the day in Zihuatanejo. After spending 24 hours a day together for nearly three weeks including our time in Manitoba, even our idiosyncrasies irritated each other. Actually, just looking at Trevor in his stupid red Coca-Cola T-shirt became annoying, never mind dealing with his inefficiency.

By now I could see that Trevor and I had different agendas to match our differing personalities. I still wanted to expedite our departure from Mexico and push as far south as time and finances would allow. Trevor preferred to make frequent and lengthy stops, an attitude he defended by citing back problems. How could I argue with that? Of course, that still didn't explain his inefficiency, or why his back suddenly seemed to bother him whenever we found a beach he liked. I hated myself for thinking that. At any rate, we were slowly becoming travel partners on a parallel trip rather than close friends on a mutual journey.

I explored the town with the freedom to move at my own pace, but with no one to share my experiences. I retreated to the hostel at night to lounge in a hammock and drink cheap Sols with other travellers. The Day of the Dead hit a macabre crescendo in the street, but we didn't care.

When you travel, there comes a time when nothing impresses you any more and you long for the familiar. I got tired of seeing churches in Europe. I got tired of temples in Egypt. That night, I was just tired of Mexico.

You see, I have this theory: travelling is like reverting to infancy. I'm not referring to the constant diarrhoea and vomiting (that would be taking the analogy too far). I mean that everything is new, everything is stressful. With each waking moment, unfamiliar sights flood your eyes, strange smells fill your nostrils, unintelligible language tickles your ears and you constantly learn, just like an infant. Is it any wonder babies just eat and sleep? Their tiny minds shut down periodically in order to process it all, much the same way a weary traveller needs to lie in a hammock and drink beer once in a while instead of seeing one more amazing sight or taking in one more cultural experience. Some of us just need more beer than others.

November 3

Trevor kept his signal light on from the hostel to the outskirts of the city. Actually, I think it had been on since signalling left out of his driveway in Canada. He must have included that in each morning's pre-trip inspection: "Chain tension, check. Tire pressure, check. Left signal light on, check."

That's not just annoying, it's a safety concern. I mean, what if somebody who didn't know Trevor as well as I did actually thought the signal meant he intended to turn? Theoretically, that driver might turn into his path, causing a horrible accident.

I always tried to alert Trevor when I noticed he had forgotten to cancel his signal. If I rode in front, I'd leave my flasher on for many, many kilometres until he got the hint. If we came to a stop sign or red light, I'd lean over and shout, "Your blinker's on!" Sometimes I'd open and close my fist in time with the flashes while riding beside him. But if Trevor rode in front of me, as he did on this day, I could do nothing but stare at that stupid, blinking light. It was hypnotic. The sound of my engine and surrounding traffic faded and disappeared. I could hear his signal flashing on and off inside my head – click-click, click-click, click-click.

We stopped to pick up a few things from a grocery store.

"Hey Trevor, your signal's been on since we left the hostel."

"Ooops," he laughed. "I keep forgetting."

"Yeah." I wasn't laughing. "So, I did a few calculations. Let's say your light flashes once every second and we average five hours of riding every day."

Trevor wasn't laughing any more.

"That's 18,000 flashes per day. Multiply that by 16 days and you know what?"

"What?" Trevor snapped.

"That's 288,000 flashes!" I yelled. "Are you waiting for the bulb to burn out? If you don't cancel your signal light you'll get yourself killed! Do I have to hook the blinker up to your horn so you remember it's on?" Of course, I was bluffing. Only Trevor knew how to do that.

Trevor stormed off while I stayed with the bikes. I felt a knot in my stomach and immediately regretted what I'd said, or rather, how I'd said it.

I oiled my chain while Trevor was away. Then I oiled Trevor's. We didn't talk when Trevor returned, but quietly kicked a few rocks in the parking lot, carefully avoiding eye contact.

"I oiled our chains," I said.

"Cool. Thanks."

"So, wha'd ya get?"

"Sun block. Do you want some?"

"I guess. I don't want you to be the only pasty white guy on this trip."

Trevor smiled.

And they say men don't communicate their feelings. What more could either of us have wanted... an apology? Trevor minded his signal light for the rest of the day, and the conflict quickly faded from consciousness.

It faded from consciousness, but not before making a subtle alteration to the dynamics between Trevor and me. Unbeknownst to us, dozens of these little arguments had created a tumour that lurked beneath the surface of our relationship. Already deeply rooted, it grew imperceptibly with every argument, weakening our bond. But we would have to deal with that later; at the moment, we had to ride.

Towards the end of a long day, we hit a line of traffic that stretched for miles into Acapulco. We parked at the back of the queue and steeled ourselves against a lengthy wait.

Just then a guy on a little scooter buzzed between Trevor and me, swerving in and out of traffic, vanishing in the crowd. Trevor looked at me. Timidly at first, then with growing audacity, we used our bikes to their fullest advantage. We rode along shoulders, through ditches, on sidewalks and between parked cars. We expected the trapped motorists would be indignant with our behaviour, but they encouraged us to squeak through tight spots and even moved their vehicles to give us a little more room. For a few moments we were heroes of the common man, symbolic of freedom and mobility – until Trevor toppled into a ditch. Trevor jumped clear and the bike came to rest upside down with its wheels spinning lethargically in the air. A passenger from a slow-moving bus hopped out and helped us drag the machine out of the narrow, concrete ditch and onto the road.

Finally, we reached the bland streets of Acapulco. A shaggy man who brought travellers to hotels for commission chased us on foot along congested roads for many blocks. If he successfully directed us to a hotel, he would receive a few pesos for his effort from the hotel manager, but the money would come out of our pockets. And, as Trevor and I had recently recalculated our budget, we knew that we needed to save every peso we could at this point. In spite of the muggy heat and the man's inappropriate footwear, he managed to stay with us as long as we remained in first gear. We pulled away from him in second gear, but he caught us when we stopped for traffic lights. He always approached, breathless, but cheerful and eager to show us a hotel. I liked his enthusiasm, but we lost him and stumbled across a cheap hotel with no help.

I went in to look at the room just as the shaggy guy sprinted around the corner, breathless. He told the proprietor that we had chosen the hotel on his recommendation. I said I had never seen the man before in my life.

November 4

Before leaving Mexico, we had to find a bank and pay for the tourist visas we'd received while entering the country. I walked up to the teller and showed him my paperwork. He began to process the transaction, but quickly ran into a problem with the rubber stamp.

The stamp had removable numbers and letters for changing the date, and one of the numbers was missing. I stood there for 15 minutes while the clerk scoured the bank for the absentee digit. Apparently, the number belonged in a tiny metal case because he kept scanning its contents, over and over. A few times he actually checked the case, closed it, and then checked it again without even putting it down; clearly, he expected the number to arrive at any moment. After each examination we exchanged confounded looks with one another, slowly shaking our heads in utter disbelief.

While I waited, Trevor came in to cash some traveller's cheques. His teller said that their computers had experienced a massive failure and that they couldn't help him. My teller said that their rubber stamp had experienced a massive failure and that they couldn't help me. However, they both agreed that they could quickly rectify the problems and we should check back momentarily.

"If they can't fix the rubber stamp, how are they going to fix the computer?" Trevor asked. I glanced over my shoulder as we left the bank to see my teller checking the metal case again. We decided to try our luck at another bank in a few days somewhere down the road.

On the way out of Acapulco, I guarded the bikes while Trevor ran into Wal-Mart to buy sunscreen. By the time he returned, I had signed us up to listen to a sales pitch on time-share vacations. Why? Because we'd gotten off to a late start and we could hit the resort on the way out of town without losing too much time, and because my weak mind had turned to putty in the hands of a fast talker who promised us each 50 US dollars to listen to the pitch.

"Hey Trev," I said, "This guy wants to give *us* money. Can you believe that?"

"Time-shares?" asked Trevor without changing expression.

"Yeah. You've heard of it?"

"Mmm-hmm. I know people who go to these things all the time."

"So it's real? They pay you to sit there for real?"

"Yeah, it's real. But it's not pleasant." Trevor thought for a bit. "I guess we could use the cash."

For the next several hours, a greasy-haired salesman with a thin moustache worked awfully hard to sell us something unwanted, unnecessary and unaffordable. He should have taken one look at us, given us 50 bucks for being sober, and then shuffled us out the back before we started panhandling by the pool.

Instead, he launched into a lengthy sales pitch laced with a complex display of confidence and desperation. He tried to demonstrate how much money we wasted by *renting* hotels when we could be *investing* in a time-share.

"So, how much money do you guys spend every night on hotels when you're on vacation?" he asked. He obviously expected to hear a large sum of money.

"I'm not sure, exactly. Maybe 18 dollars per night," I said.

"Wow. Okay, so that's pretty good." He looked stunned for a moment, but decided to run with it anyway. He took out a pencil and started doing the math.

"Still, that's 18 dollars per night each, so..."

"Actually, that's between the two of us. It's more like nine dollars each per night," said Trevor. I nodded. This guy was dealing with people who considered toilet seats a luxury.

In the end, we escaped without investing anything but time and we gained 50 dollars each. But first we'd had to convince three people in different levels of management that we would not purchase a time-share for any price, time or planet.

Our maps showed a little town called San Marcos about 60 kilometres down the road and we figured we could make it before dark. We assumed we could find accommodation there; an impressively large dot represented the town on our maps.

I rode in front and, as per strict guidelines set forth in my modus operandi, sped directly through our destination without slowing down. Trevor, who nearly always paid attention to such details as our current location, signalled me to turn around.

It seemed that San Marcos had only one hotel. The decrepit building contained three dirty, concrete rooms, but no guests. Soiled mattresses sagged under their own weight on creaky, metal beds. Bare light bulbs hung from the ceiling and flickered as though someone was being electrocuted in another room. The old landlord demanded 200 pesos per night, underscoring the fact that he owned the only hotel in the vicinity.

"Oh man. I don't want to stay here," I said. "But I don't think we have a choice." Trevor shook his head.

The sun had gone down while we inspected the rooms in stunned silence.

"200 pesos is too much for this dump," said Trevor.

"Yeah, but this guy's the only game in town. He doesn't have to bargain."

"Maybe we should pretend to leave. See if the price drops then."

"Yeah. Man, this guy lives in squalor, he has three empty rooms… he should drop the price when he sees us leaving."

We frowned and shook our heads. We put our helmets on and started the bikes. "180 pesos?" I shouted over the thumping of our engines. The landlord remained indifferent. We planned to ride away slowly, providing ample time for the landlord to chase after us and make a counter-offer. To complete our bluff, we turned towards San Marcos along the darkened highway for one last, hopeless search for accommodations, certain that we would have to return to the dumpy hotel and pay the landlord's exorbitant rent.

To our amazement, we found another hotel, a hotel that provided cleaner and more affordable accommodation. A transport truck had obscured the entrance when we'd driven past earlier, but we could see the sign riding the other way.

San Marcos was actually bigger than it appeared from the highway and we strolled down a long street lined with shops towards the centre of town after supper. We found a wide public square and sat on one of the concrete benches in front of a colonial church. Without agenda or destination, people strolled through the busy square beneath electric lights, simply enjoying the heat of the night and each other's company. In Canada, all of these people would be in front of their televisions by now.

We became the centre of attention once some teenagers worked up the courage to talk to us. In the end, a large group of boys and two girls gathered around us to practice their English. They even took pictures of us.

November 5

I felt uneasy at the breakfast table. The restaurant was fine, we were on schedule, the weather was okay, but I had a bad vibe. Moments before sitting down to order, Trevor and I had fuelled up our bikes. I'd needed 83 pesos in fuel. I thought I'd given the attendant 200, but I'd only collected 17 in change. To be honest, I couldn't recall how much I'd given the guy. In Canada, you just fork over the money and expect correct change. When travelling you have to be more careful. I suppose you should be more careful in Canada, too. The more I thought about it, the more convinced I became that the gas attendant had ripped me off.

While Trevor waited for our food I raced back to the station, roaring up to the offender and yelling, "*Necesito uno más cien.*" In my haste I neglected to lift the visor on my helmet and it sounded like I was shouting through a pillow. "*¿Qué?*" he asked. I lifted the visor and repeated slowly, "*Necesito uno más cien.*" I'm not sure what that means exactly, but the phrase contains the key words "need," "more" and "hundred."

The chubby attendant threw a sheepish glance at his current customer and quickly handed me 100 pesos. He said that I'd taken off before he could give me my change. He was lying, of course, but I lacked the Spanish vocabulary to yell at him properly. I glared at him for a while and shook my head in a "your mother would be ashamed" sort of way before riding back for breakfast.

I don't remember much of the ride that day except for our encounters with wildlife. We saw many iguanas, tarantulas and buzzards. Now that I think of it, the buzzards seemed to be following us; I'm not sure what that means. Apart from the buzzards, the birds in Mexico display amazing colour and sing such beautiful songs. One particularly colourful bird slammed off Trevor's helmet in a cloud of feathers at a closing speed of approximately 160 kilometres per hour.

November 6

We rented a private cabin near the beach in Puerto Escondido, a town renowned for its surfing. Pink mosquito nets, tied in large overhand knots to keep them from touching the wooden floor, hung above each bed from varnished beams of deep red wood. After breakfast we rode around looking for surfboard rentals.

Our search was unsuccessful, but I didn't care. We had too much fun ripping around, unencumbered by luggage or helmets. We tore up some dirt roads and along deserted beaches, popping little wheelies and spinning our back tires like a couple of kids.

We returned to the cabin around noon. Trevor's bike had developed a mysterious noise that made him uncomfortable and he wanted to research the problem on the Internet. I lounged by the pool and read.

Earlier, we'd met a couple of Germans who had bought a GMC Jimmy in California. Max and Jojo hoped to drive the truck to the southern tip of Chile, surfing popular breaks along the way. At one in the afternoon, Jojo stumbled out of his cabin and offered to let me use his surfboard.

During the previous night, after a bottle of tequila and some off-road racing, the pair had high centred their Jimmy on a sand dune. The local police helped them extricate the vehicle, but had demanded 2,500 pesos in exchange for their freedom. The cops kept Jojo as collateral while Max drove, drunk, to a cash machine. Suffice it to say, they'd had a late night and didn't feel like surfing.

They say the longer the board, the easier to learn. Jojo was a seasoned surfing veteran; he had a short board. Short boards are great for quick turns and stunts, but they need speed to stay above the water. Long boards are sluggish, but buoyant. By my estimation, Jojo's board, the one I was using for my first surfing experience, should have been about 200 feet longer.

Still, I strutted along the beach with the board under my arm, confident in my ability to learn and look good simultaneously. I placed the board on the sand and practiced *popping* from my stomach to my feet in one smooth motion, a technique I learned from the movie *Point Break*.

Now, jumping up and down on a surfboard attracts attention. A small crowd gathered to watch me catch my first wave. I waded into the surf, holding the board like a pro. I walked in up to my waist, and then turned to see if my little audience was still watching. They smiled and waved. I turned back to the ocean, suddenly aware that I would catch my first wave sooner than I expected.

Instinctively I raised the surfboard like a shield against 10,000 pounds of raging water, an experience I liken to carrying a sheet of plywood through a tornado. I landed neatly at the feet of my Mexican admirers. "*Mucho bueno*," they laughed. Then they took pictures of me.

I took a few moments to recover and exchange pleasantries with the peanut gallery before heading back into the water. The next surge serendipitously deposited my body at the feet of three attractive ladies wearing nothing but tiny bikini bottoms. Unfortunately, my conversational skills are no better in Spanish than English, and I may have had a mild concussion that made the situation worse.

"*Estoy cansado*," I sputtered. "*Surfing es difícil.*"

The girls looked at me with vacuous smiles, a response I've grown accustomed to. I paddled back into the surf to meet my doom.

I finally caught a wave and managed to ride it on my feet. Rather, I struggled to a squatting position as the board lost momentum and sank beneath my weight to the sand, just six inches below the water. I remained squatting for a moment on the submerged board, fully aware that this might forever be the crowning achievement of my surfing career.

Trevor showed up and I gave him the surfboard. Then I just lay on the beach and watched girls before returning home to do laundry and make coffee.

After I left, Trevor met some ladies from Montréal and arranged to meet them that evening. Conversations with beautiful women came easy for Trevor if he approached them alone. If he had my "help," events unfolded something like this.

On days where I managed uncharacteristic restraint, I'd actually wait until someone addressed me, or at least made eye contact, before blurting out, "WE'RE TRAVELLING BY MOTORBIKE!" Then, suddenly reminded that conversations founded on egotistic non sequitur are beyond salvage, I'd hum quietly to myself while smiling and nodding at whatever banal chit-chat spewed forth from Trevor. I'm exaggerating (slightly), but there are times I wonder how I've managed to function in society as long as I have.

November 8

My skin tingled under a hot sun as waves of a thousand searing pinpricks washed over my body. We rode on through a landscape of prickly scrub brush and sand that reflected the heat, stopping intermittently to seek shade and drink as much water as possible. Later in the day, the weather cooled as thick, dark clouds veiled the sun, but the wind became our oppressor. We rode too long, too late, and passed the last real hope of finding decent accommodation. A small town and tiny hotel would have to do.

We became the only guests in Niltepec's singular hotel, a hotel that remained under construction. A pair of German shepherds managed site security, silently roaming the grounds, slipping in and out of shadows and scaring the crap out of us.

Niltepec consists of three or four perfectly straight streets perpendicular to the highway. The paved streets, connected by a grid of gravel lanes, run for several kilometres.

The taxi service consists of bicycles with trailers decked out in flashing red lights. Perhaps the city planners had these guys in mind when they designed the place. Either that or they intended to build an airstrip and people just settled there.

November 9

We awoke to the sound of heavy rain. It rained while we packed. It rained while we cooked breakfast and then, as we prepared to ride into the rain, it stopped. It cleared so well that I decided to ride in jeans and a T-shirt. Trevor chose to remain decked out in full rain gear, which made me feel much better about my decision. Somehow, Trevor always managed to predict the weather accurately for the day, and then select the most outrageously inappropriate riding gear for it. The weather turned hot and Trevor had to remove some layers just a few kilometres from where we'd started.

We pulled over at a military checkpoint on the main highway known as the Mex 200. Usually the soldiers just asked to see the papers for our bikes and our passports before waving us through. This time, they searched us.

I got the distinct impression that the soldiers conducted these slipshod inspections to alleviate boredom. A young soldier reached into a zippered pocket on my backpack and withdrew a handful of Canadian change. He rolled a small copper coin between his thumb and forefinger, curiously examining the twin maple leaves worn smooth by years of circulation. He turned his attention to another coin with a shiny silver schooner.

"Canadian," I said. The soldier nodded, still examining the coins.

"For you," I said. It seemed wise to keep the guys with guns smiling, and it only cost 11 cents. To my surprise, he handed me ten pesos in exchange and wished me a good trip.

Trevor and I fired up our bikes with the push of a button. Some of the soldiers looked confused and mimicked the motion of a kick-start engine with their legs. Obviously impressed with the machines, they suddenly wanted to see us do wheelies. They raised imaginary handlebars above their heads, and pointed at the highest number on our speedometers, then at us.

Now, the highest number on the speedometer of a KLR 650, measured in kilometres, is 180. The guy in charge of speedometer design for Kawasaki either had little communication with the engineers, or badly misinterpreted what they told him about the machine. Then again, numbers on motorcycle speedometers are notoriously arbitrary. Larger numbers indicate a higher rate of speed than smaller numbers, but accuracy never factors into the equation. They might as well make speedometers with the symbol of a rabbit and turtle to indicate fast and slow, like old John Deere lawn tractors.

I'm not sure what would happen if I ever tried to bury the needle on my speedometer, but I imagine I would be vibrated into unconsciousness long before I succeeded. I pointed to a more reasonable number – 80 – and nodded my head, hoping to convince the soldiers that we would never violate traffic laws in their fine country. They knew as well as I did that the only traffic law in Mexico was an abridged version of *The Origin of Species*.

After leaving the soldiers, we abandoned the Mex 200 for a road that twisted into the mountains towards San Cristóbal through a turbulent wind. The road changed direction often and dramatically, first punching us through walls of wind and then dropping us into pockets of dead air. In these sudden moments of complete calm, I could have balanced a birthday cupcake on my helmet and the wind wouldn't have blown out the candle.

The wind subsided as we climbed higher. Clouds spilled though cracks in the mountains above us like silent tsunamis breaking in slow motion. Soon we were in their midst. Though it never rained exactly, the mist deceived us into thinking we didn't need rain gear and then soaked us to the bone.

Occasionally, the sun pierced the clouds to warm our bodies and spotlight the breathtaking scenery. Rounding one particularly sharp, rising corner, I looked back down on the road we had just ascended. Its wet surface reflected the sun like a brilliant silver ribbon weaving through the mist and the deep, green mountains.

Trevor and I happened upon a dark but neat little restaurant in San Cristóbal that operated entirely with a staff of two men. A three-foot wall separated the kitchen and dining area. We took a table next to the little wall and were immediately attended to by half of the restaurant's employees. He took our order while the other half of the employees stood behind the wall and pretended not to overhear.

The waiter brought me a delicate white cup of rich coffee. I cradled the warm cup in my hands, letting it siphon the chill from my fingers.

November 10

A small avalanche of paper, tape, string and cardboard settled on the counter of the post office in San Cristóbal. I blinked expectantly at the postmaster over the pile of material and he glared back at me. With a heavy sigh, he stomped away and called for a perky young girl to attend to my mailing needs. She patiently packaged my film, wrapped it in tape and told me to label the contents clearly on the box. It cost me 78 pesos to mail four rolls of film to Canada.

As coincidence would have it, and unbeknownst to me, Trevor had been sending film to Canada that day and irritating the very same postal worker, which explained a lot. The same people charged him 62 pesos, informed him that tape is not allowed on the package and that he should not label the contents on the exterior.

This illustrates a significant problem. Understanding rapid-fire Spanish instructions and making distinctions between similar phrases such as "you must not use a box," and "you must not neglect to use a box," can be quite difficult. The consequences of misunderstanding such instructions are usually negligible, but imagine this scenario: Trevor and I stop to inquire as to the safety of a certain road. Trevor hears, "Use this road. It is not dangerous," and I hear, "Don't use this road. It is dangerous." That's not good.

And, speaking of which, we'd heard rumours that danger lurked on the road from San Cristóbal to Tapachula. Armed bandits supposedly patrolled the road, which skirted the Mexican border with Guatemala. From experience, Trevor and I knew that such rumours were typically inaccurate, but I decided to make inquiries. I stopped at several information centres, where I learned that the bandits had long ago hung up their guns. At least, that's what I think I was told.

November 11

We crammed into a white minivan with a dozen strangers and took a tour of some waterfalls en route to the Mayan ruins of Palenque. As I jumped out of the van, I noticed a path leading into the deluge behind the massive falls. Before I could resist, a small part of my brain had me stripping off my shirt and running headlong into the torrent.

For the remainder of the cramped van ride, I experienced levels of discomfort typically reserved for mountaineers and Indian holy men. My jeans smelled strangely similar to urine as the water evaporated, fogging up the windows and creating a cloud of self-consciousness that hung over my head as I sat chafing. It was a relief to finally arrive at the ruins and escape the van.

Palenque's majestic ruins rise naturally from the jungle as if they had always existed: discovered by man, not created. Of course, it's absurd to think something so orderly had no creator, but given the seamless blend of forest and hewn stone, one could easily entertain such a notion… if only for a short while.

Terraced stone pyramids with wide steps, worn smooth by centuries of rain and millions of rubber-soled sneakers, tower above the forest canopy, offering sweeping views of fertile plains. Cream-coloured temples, towers and courtyards look down on manicured lawns that end abruptly at the edge of the jungle.

We climbed a winding flight of stone steps and sat down in the shade to rest and take in the view. A few senior citizens from the United States wandered past. A couple of them sat down with us and struck up a conversation. They told us about their group bus tour of Mexico, and we told them that we'd travelled from Canada on motorbikes.

"Wow, that must be nice," said the old man. His wife nodded. "That's real freedom."

"Yeah," I said, "but it comes with a price. We can go where we want and when we want, but we're always concerned with security and maintenance."

"I hadn't thought about that," the man said. His wife nodded again. "But you can go at your own pace. You can just go. When you're in a big group travelling by bus, it seems you're always waiting for one slow person."

"Yeah, it's the same when there are two of you travelling by motorbike."

I said it before I could stop myself. I didn't look at Trevor, but I could feel him tense up. We all laughed, but for different reasons.

Later, as Trevor and I stood atop one of the ancient, stone structures, we heard an eerie sound coming from the jungle. The deep, haunting scream sent a chill down the length of my spine. The cry sounded tortured, angry and mournful. I vaguely recalled it from the *National Geographic* Channel.

"What's that noise?" Trevor asked as he turned his gaze to the trees.

"I think they're howler monkeys," I replied, suddenly placing the sound in my memory.

"It sounds like machinery of some kind," said Trevor.

"Yeah, kind of. But I think they're howler monkeys."

"They must be building something."

"I'm quite sure howler monkeys make that noise."

"Or maybe they have a stage set up and are putting on some kind of weird play."

"Howler monkeys."

"Maybe just some kids screaming."

A tour guide walked by.

"Excuse me," I said, glancing over at Trevor to make sure he was paying attention. "What's that sound?"

"Monkeys," said the guide.

"What kind?" asked Trevor.

I stared at him for a moment.

"They're freaking HOWLER MONKEYS," I yelled and stormed into the jungle. Trevor would admit the stupid sound came from stupid monkeys if it killed me. We thrashed around in the bush for a while, but our enthusiasm to investigate diminished the closer we got to the howling. It's not an inviting sound.

November 12

I loaded my bags in the street outside our hostel while Trevor retrieved luggage from our room. As I struggled to secure a difficult strap, I knocked my machine onto its side with a loud crash. I desperately wrestled the bike to its wheels just in time to strike a casual pose and whistle an innocent tune before Trevor appeared in the doorway, none the wiser. However, he arrived just in time to see my helmet, placed hastily on my seat, fall and bounce off the cobblestone – a move that had sort of become my trademark.

"You have to be more careful with your bucket," said Trevor a little irritably.

"I know," I said as I picked up the helmet and examined its new scars.

We rolled away from San Cristóbal after saying goodbye to our friends at the hostel. Leaving the cold weather high in the mountains, we descended the road that led south on the Mexican side of the Guatemalan border.

Mexican roads are usually narrower than Canadian roads. Still, when we came upon a snake that stretched from the shoulder to the centre line, it looked impressive. We estimated the black beast to be at least eight feet long. The snake slithered into the tall grass as Trevor and I stopped our bikes for a closer look. We shuffled to the edge of the vegetation, each trying to use the other as a shield.

"Should we go in after it?" I asked, poking the grass with a long stick.

Trevor looked at me and smiled. I knew exactly what he was thinking.

Trevor and I had met in Austria at a mountaineering school in 1995. The school mainly attracted North American boys, and in our minds, we would frolic with golden-haired Austrian maidens in alpine meadows under the soft caress of summer sun. Unfortunately, the director viewed the school's curriculum in a different light.

Following an ambiguous orientation and several stupid icebreaker games, we relinquished our watches to the powers that be (there is no time in hell) and stumbled into the mountains under the cover of darkness. Ulli, our lanky German guide, had shaggy black hair and a beard that looked as if it might try to escape. He never quite found pants capable of concealing his ankles, nor the correct English phrase for any idea he wished to express, but his quiet, gentle nature made him a pleasant companion.

Our little band of intrepid adventurers whiled away many wonderful days in the Austrian Alps, climbing, caving and hiking under Ulli's watchful eye. Against all odds, a seed of romance sprouted between me and a beautiful girl from Ontario. Yes, I had reached a pinnacle in my young life and it seemed as though things could not possibly get better.

Of course, pinnacles are precarious. I learned that lesson while hiking through an alpine meadow alive with wildflowers and velvet grass. Our group stumbled across a lethargic little snake sunning itself along the path.

The animal reminded me of the common garter snakes found on the Canadian prairies, harmless really – the kind of snakes little boys capture to torment little girls on lazy summer Sundays. Suddenly, I had a brilliant idea: I would seize the beast and impress the Ontario girl with my bravery.

Long before Ulli could articulate an English objection, I stumbled forward and grabbed the serpent behind its head. From my limited experience with garter snakes, I knew that if I caught the animal just so, it would be unable to turn and strike. Then again, garter snakes seldom bite even when handled improperly, and this little monster quickly demonstrated agility and aggression far superior to any garter snake I had ever improperly handled. Without hesitation, it unleashed a blood-chilling hiss and, with all the cervical trickery of a great horned owl, spun its head completely around, piercing my left thumb with a fang that seemed improbably long for such a small creature.

I caught the snake to impress a girl. Mission accomplished. My new goal (detaching myself from the hissing snake that dangled from my thumb by one fang) proved more difficult. I held the reptile at shoulder height with an outstretched arm while considering my options. I thought about grabbing it by the tail and ripping it out of my flesh, but that seemed intuitively unwise.

The only alternative – the one I chose – was panic, and it came more naturally. I hopped around shaking my arm and screaming like an eight-year-old boy playing kissing tag at recess. Finally, the snake dropped to the ground and slithered away, shaken, but unharmed.

Ulli followed me for the rest of the afternoon, nervously breaking the silence every few minutes to ask how I felt. I felt embarrassed. Also, my swollen thumb had turned purple and begun throbbing with a dull pain. Eventually the pain crept into my hand, then my elbow, then my shoulder.

"This isn't funny any more," said Ulli when the venom finally reached its icy fingers into my neck and jaw, implying that he had recently been amused. He radioed for Hans Peter, the director, who arrived suddenly and silently, as though carried by the wind.

A wiry, Austrian mountaineer with stereotypical blond hair and piercing blue eyes, Hans Peter spoke softly, but with intimidating authority. He conveyed a certain quiet assurance that his masculinity lay beyond reproach; like most Austrian men, he could wear an outfit that included tight leather shorts with suspenders, wool socks hiked up to the knee and a frilly pastel shirt with embroidered flowers while still managing to look tough. He had a sort of air about him, like a father figure, that made you seek his approval. I'll never forget his first words to me.

"Jeremy, you idiot."

"That's just what my mom used to say," I stammered.

"What were you thinking?" he pressed, and waited for an answer.

Now, a guy like me gets asked that question an awful lot over the course of his life. I have never really answered it to anyone's complete satisfaction. Honesty is never the right tack, nor is humour, although I briefly considered saying, "I collect venom." In the end I believe I said nothing, invariably the correct response.

Hans Peter marched me away from Ulli and my friends, some of whom wished me a melodramatic final farewell. After a few minutes of hurried hiking, we found a tiny alpine hut inhabited by two elderly but sturdy women. Hans Peter explained the situation to them – undoubtedly underscoring that I was an idiot – and the women sprung into action while clucking their tongues and worriedly shaking their heads.

One woman poured me a glass of warm milk and the other spread a clean blanket over her bed for me. Then they left with Hans Peter. Before he shut the door he turned to me and said in the most impressively callous manner, "People have been killed by snakes in this region. You might die." With that, he closed the door and left me alone with my thoughts.

I lay in a one-room shack with a small entryway and adjoining pantry. The shack, built from weathered, rough-hewn timber, had no frivolous decorations except for a bouquet of wildflowers on the wooden table and a lacy white curtain for the room's only window.

I rested on the bed and wondered if some of the last words I would ever hear might be, "Jeremy, you idiot. You might die."

I thought about dying. I'd always put on a brave face when the subject came up in conversation, but this was the first time I had ever confronted the possibility of death. I prayed a bit, but not for healing – just that my mom would be comforted if I did die. As it turned out, I felt fully prepared to cross that river, shuffle off this mortal coil, kick the bucket, buy the farm… but I digress.

After coming up with countless euphemisms for death, and following immeasurable moments of self-reflection (moments immeasurable because the school still had my watch) it occurred to me that I had no idea what would happen next. Hans Peter had been somewhat vague regarding the details.

As I thought about this I heard the deep thumping of rotary wings beating the air in the distance. The thumping grew louder as the helicopter drew near, labouring for purchase in the thin alpine air. I stepped outside to watch the cumbersome military machine set down in the meadow, as if the pilot were loath to crush any wildflowers. I boarded the machine and waved to Hans Peter as we lifted off – to my great relief, he smiled and waved back.

Though the flight to Shladming lasted a mere four minutes, I had a lot of time to think. It occurred to me that my grasp of the German language might prove inadequate when faced with a medical emergency. Eager to amuse myself and confuse the locals, the very first thing I'd learned to say in German was, "I am a pretty village." I'd quickly added other expressions to my useless German arsenal, such as, "You are a platypus" and "I have a bunion." Unfortunately, my linguistic prowess had not significantly increased since my arrival in Austria.

The helicopter touched down, deposited me neatly at the hospital's emergency ward and flew off, likely to rescue some other idiot on another mountain. Doctors and nurses rallied around me shouting at each other in German – the words "platypus" and "bunion" conspicuous in their absence.

They rushed me to a sterile room with bright lights and placed me on a metal table. A doctor shouted orders to my growing medical team and then hurried out of the room with his stethoscope swinging wildly about his neck. Judging by their reactions, I imagine that he instructed his staff to make a lot of noise and run about looking busy.

The hospital staff's high level of emotion and activity became unsustainable. The room quieted down and my crack medical team shuffled off without having really done anything. Seizing this opportunity, a male nurse unsheathed the single largest needle I have ever seen and prepared to deliver a mighty blow to my bare buttocks.

He appeared to be acting alone on this decision and I briefly considered calling for help, but I could only shout, "I am a pretty village." I believe the nurse backed up a few paces to get a run at me and then stood with the needle in his hand, windmilling his arm for dramatic effect – but that may be a distortion in my memory. At the last possible moment a doctor returned, shouted at him angrily and snatched the syringe from his hand.

For three days I stayed in hospital, unable to communicate with patients or staff. I sought solace in the pages of an English Bible and committed to memory Jeremiah 8:17, which reads, "'See, I will send venomous snakes among you, vipers that cannot be charmed, and they will bite you,' declares the LORD."

At the end of my solitary confinement, the hospital released me and Ulli came to pick me up. The pain in my arm remained, and would linger for another month. Although I never received any actual treatment, the hospital bill came to 2,000 Canadian dollars – including the helicopter ride.

Ulli smiled as we got into his car and said, "I'm glad to see you're all right. Now Hans Peter has another story to tell."

Trevor likes to tell the story, too. He made some wise-ass crack about Mexican helicopters and we rode away, leaving the snake in peace.

We approached a small town guarded by *topes*. Essentially, *topes* are highway-sized speed bumps that manifest themselves either as parallel rows of metal hemispheres the size of cloven softballs, or large, rounded humps of asphalt.

No matter what variety, *topes* have no effect on speeders with high travel-suspension motorcycles. Trevor and I often blew the doors off half a dozen vehicles when they slowed to navigate the bumps.

As I neared the *topes*, I pulled out to pass a bus belching thick exhaust. At that exact moment, the bus pulled out to pass an even slower vehicle. I suddenly faced a dilemma: leaving the road by way of a nasty drop to my left, or completing the pass.

I dropped a gear and cracked the throttle wide open, easing the bike as close to the edge of the road as I thought possible. I made brief eye contact with the bus driver in his mirror. I could see him shaking his head and cursing but, like me, he had already committed to passing the car in front of him. The next few seconds seemed to take a long time. As the bus edged closer, I drifted towards the ditch, accelerating hard. I escaped the crash literally by centimetres.

After a few kilometres I pulled over to wait for Trevor, who remained stuck behind traffic. I averted my gaze from the bus driver as he roared past, and I was still shaking when Trevor caught up to me.

"Didn't you see his signal light?" Trevor asked.

Indeed I had. It said *Made in Taiwan*. Also, the question seemed odd, considering Trevor displayed no discernable link between signalling and turning. I said nothing.

The road climbed and fell through beautiful mountains and twisted alongside a river that had carved a deep gorge for itself. At the end of the day we had regained nearly all of the elevation we'd lost leaving San Cristóbal, the highway having delivered us to Motozintla de Mendoza.

Our maps confirmed what the road signs indicated: a mere 50 kilometres stood between us and our destination of Tapachula, an international transportation hub near the Pacific Ocean. Our maps also hinted that we could expect to lose up to 1,900 metres in elevation along the way. Every local we spoke with said we should expect the drive to take two hours. We'd never make it before dark.

While Trevor searched for a room on foot, I guarded the bikes and made friends in the street. I stumbled through a long conversation with one particularly patient shopkeeper whose store I had effectively barricaded with my motorbike. Still, she spoke kindly and slowly to me, simply nodding when I answered questions that she hadn't asked.

Trevor found a great deal on lodging, and we decided to spoil ourselves and get a room with its own private bathroom for an extra 30 pesos. After supper we hung out in a public square where we practised our Spanish on the locals and they practised their English on us.

Half a dozen little boys carrying shoeshine boxes swarmed us and offered their services. I wanted to hire them, but they would have ruined my runners with their polish. The boys seemed very young: I guessed ages ranging from six to ten. When we asked them their age, they all said nine. Every one of them claimed to be nine years old. Some of the boys obviously lied to us, either because kids like messing with foreigners or there's a labour law stipulating that shoeshine boys must be at least nine to solicit business in a public square.

What a contrast between their childhood and mine. When I was nine, my biggest concern was waking up in time to watch the Smurfs before hockey practice, followed by how to take a leak after putting on all my hockey equipment over my jeans.

November 13

According to plan we would enter another country the next day, and none too soon in my opinion. There must have been a prominent Mexican architect who stood four feet tall at one time, because most doorways in the country measure five and a half feet high. As Trevor and I both stand about six feet tall, we developed thick calluses on our heads from incessantly thumping into concrete doorjambs.

Following the tortured flow of a writhing river, we headed south from Motozintla de Mendoza along a road that clung to steep banks. The deep gorge, cloaked in the shade of an impenetrable forest canopy, dropped sharply from the mountains to the sea and provided the perfect playground for a switchback competition between river and road. Our bikes sat high, so it surprised me when my toe inadvertently dragged on the pavement while leaning into some of the tight corners.

In spite of the previous day's close call with the bus, we continued passing vehicles as they slowed for *topes*. We jumped ahead of a green VW bug, but as soon as the car cleared the bumps it took off like a shot and caught us within a few short moments. The car had a low, aggressive stance and possibly a racing suspension, because we couldn't pull away from it in the corners. We rode harder and faster than usual, winding our engines into their upper limits just to stay in front of Herbie the Love Bug's malevolent offspring.

Whenever I slowed for a corner the bug practically snapped at my back tire. I struggled to keep in front of him while pushing Trevor through the corners. The three of us yo-yoed down the curvy road as if we were connected by rubber bands. The speeds reached ridiculous proportions and it seemed only a matter of time before one of the rubber bands would snap, shooting someone off the road to his doom. Trevor must have been thinking the same thing because he quickly pulled over when I flashed my lights at him, allowing the bug to pass.

However, foolish male pride being what it is, the race continued for many kilometres as Trevor and I monopolized the view in the bug's rear-view mirror. Eventually we slowed to our regular pace and let the car edge out of sight.

Leaving the thick shade of the mountains, we arrived in the hot land of multi-lane highways. The highway ran straight for want of obstacles, making up with efficiency what it lacked in appeal. Several guys at the side of the road waving laminated identification tags flagged us down. We stopped when they practically threw themselves in our path.

The ID badges these guys brandished could have been crafted by any kid in grade six with access to pencil crayons and a photocopier. Before we left Canada, Trevor and I had made several fake copies of our driver's licenses. If a corrupt cop or border official ever tried to hold the license for ransom, we could simply abandon it and extricate ourselves from the situation. Anyway, our fake licenses looked far more official than the badges these guys waved in our faces.

Shouting together and panting from the chase, they informed us that we had to cancel the import papers for our motorcycles at an office on the other side of the highway. They told us that we couldn't process the papers at the border. Of course they wanted a small fee in return for this information, and the whole process seemed rather suspicious.

First of all, the border to Guatemala was still at least 25 kilometres away and we planned to spend the night on the Mexican side in Tapachula. Cancelling our import papers a whole day before leaving the country seemed unreasonable. Secondly, if the import papers needed to be cancelled as a prerequisite for exiting the country, it was only logical that the work could be done at the border. Thirdly, it seemed unlikely that the government would delegate the responsibility of flagging down foreign vehicles to a couple of guys beside the road with laminated badges. And finally, Trevor had carefully researched border procedures on the Internet and in several guidebooks. Tapachula was a popular crossing, and nowhere had he read that we should cancel our papers 25 kilometres and one day before leaving Mexico. None of it made sense and, after talking it through over the continual shouts and pleas of the badge boys, we decided to leave them in the dust and carry on to Tapachula.

While searching for a room, Trevor's bike mysteriously toppled onto his helmet, which he had placed on the ground.

"You should be more careful with your helmet," I said. Since Trevor hadn't witnessed me dropping my bike, which I'd done twice in Canada and once in San Cristóbal, I could afford a smug little smile as I helped him lift his fallen ride. In reality, the score was tied at three drops apiece. And, just in case you were wondering, dropping the bike is both potentially bad for the machine and sort of a badge of shame for the rider. Trevor felt bad about his helmet, so I broke down and told him about my drops.

We took refuge in a cheap hotel just as the sky opened up and unleashed a downpour. Wet flakes of paint and plaster fell from the ceiling, and water trickled down the walls as we watched the storm and ensuing flood from our dingy room. I wondered if the roof might collapse.

I wondered if my partnership with Trevor might collapse, too. Lately we had been arguing more than talking, and ignoring each other more than arguing. Resentment had begun to set in, resentment over who controlled our agenda. Fortunately we shared one clear goal: to spend some weeks in Guatemala studying Spanish. About that, at least, we could agree. The storm let up as quickly as it began and we took to the streets to find supper.

November 14

The attendant filled my tank, pointed to the pesos display and quickly cleared the pump. It took me a second to realize that he had pointed to a different pump than the one I had used. All the pumps were clear now and I had no way of proving how much fuel went into my tank, but I had a good idea.

By now, I had memorized an adequate arsenal of angry phrases to yell when he told me I owed 100 pesos more than I should. He lowered the price by 50 pesos and I yelled a little softer. He finally quoted a reasonable price and I paid him. He short-changed me by five pesos, but I was just too tired to care. Why do locals always assume foreigners are idiots?

From our research we knew that border crossings in Central America could take hours. We planned to arrive at the frontier early and well prepared. Thinking it a good idea to have Guatemalan currency, we stood outside a bank with a dozen people and waited for it to open. I ran back to the bikes for a moment to double check our locks and found everyone inside the bank when I returned.

Two sets of glass doors allowed access to the building. I opened the outside door and proceeded to the next set of doors, but I couldn't pull them open. Rattling the door drew the attention of everyone inside. Slightly embarrassed, I tried pushing the door. It was either stuck or locked. I pulled at another door and then pushed at it, growing more frustrated and embarrassed with each moment.

I looked helplessly at the people inside. They mimed instructions, pointing and signalling with complicated hand gestures. I seldom watch baseball on TV, but I could tell that everyone wanted me to bunt. Soothing chimes rang from a little speaker above my head, accompanied by a calm Mexican lady repeating an unintelligible message. I bounced around my little glass cell like a frenzied chimp, rattling the doors and imploring the audience to go for help. Through the glass I could see Trevor laughing and motioning for me to bunt – a motion that I began to mimic. That pleased everyone. The crowd nodded approval and bunted the air with me. For a precious moment we were all united in our love for bunting and I felt a genuine connection with the people inside. However, this triumph of cross-cultural communication failed to improve the situation, as I remained trapped.

Suddenly, another man appeared in my cell from outside the bank. At least now I had a companion with whom to live out my days, I thought. I smiled at him and motioned for him to bunt. He nodded in understanding and, grabbing the handle of the outer door (in much the same way a batter might hold a bat if he was bunting), gave it a gentle tug to close it, thereby unlocking the inner door.

I expected a round of applause from the crowd as I entered the bank, but all I heard was the sound of shuffling paper, Trevor's laughter, and one or two muffled coughs. The local audience had rightly assumed that I was a foreign idiot and turned their attention to other matters.

We waited in line for a long time to learn that the bank did not exchange currency. I decided to get pesos in the hope that I could exchange them for quetzals at the border.

Once we got out of the bank and headed towards Guatemala, everything went like clockwork... that is, until an angry mob near the border forced us off the highway. Now, I understand that people tend to be overly critical of mobs and, to be fair, they are not always angry. However, as I observed this particular mob shouting at us, shaking their fists and chasing us through angular streets lined with unremarkable houses, I couldn't help but categorize them as stereotypical, and stereotypical mobs are angry. For the time being, they remained neatly contained within the circular frames of my mirrors, but every street we tried seemed to dead-end, forcing us to turn and ride through the approaching masses. Suddenly our options were limited; they had us surrounded.

As far as angry mobs go, these guys appeared orderly and well dressed. They burned no flags, carried no torches and touted no political banners. Rather, they brandished calculators and thick wads of soft Guatemalan currency. In our ignorance we had been corralled by black market money changers.

I've always avoided these guys. Money exchanged on the street is apt to be counterfeit, and the tourist is especially vulnerable, as he is often unfamiliar with the look and feel of genuine currency. By way of example, I once received 40 dollars worth of counterfeit currency in Jordan from a man referring to himself as *The Desert Fox*. (There's another lesson – never trade money with a man named like a G.I. Joe character.)

Here again, I didn't even know what quetzals looked like. Unfortunately, it seemed as though the black market offered the only way to change money at this point. I bartered for the best exchange I could get and changed most of my Mexican cash into Guatemalan. I was ready to roll.

"I don't have any money to change," said Trevor.

"Didn't you get pesos at the bank this morning?" I asked.

Trevor shook his head and glanced around for another bank.

"Do you think these guys take traveller's cheques?" he asked.

I quietly waited for his own words to sink into his brain.

Trevor needed money. We backtracked ten kilometres to the nearest town to look for a bank. We returned to the border at 10:15 a.m., and Trevor at last changed his money on the black market.

The first step to border crossing involved a passport check. To our dismay, but not surprise, the guards informed us that we needed to return to Tapachula and get our motorcycle import papers cancelled – as we'd been told yesterday. Apparently you should always listen to guys with laminated badges who flag you down on the side of the road. It seems the technology used in lamination is so difficult to access in Mexico that only high-ranking government employees have badges covered in shiny plastic.

We turned around and headed for Tapachula, exchanging friendly waves of recognition with the men of the black market currency exchange. The road towards Tapachula was fast becoming familiar and we were able to ride it at increasing rates of speed, a skill we had to develop further if we hoped to cross into Guatemala by nightfall.

Arriving at Tapachula, we discovered that the city efficiently funnels people from Mexico to Guatemala while restricting access to motorists going the other way. We became trapped in a maze of one-way streets and roundabouts. I think we demonstrated remarkable perseverance in the face of adversity, finally emerging on the other side of town and happily riding away from our original destination.

In the heat of a midday sun, the concrete buildings of the customs office beamed like an overexposed photo. After we'd waited outside for an hour, the 15 minutes we spent in a small air-conditioned room to collect the requisite stamps seemed a little slice of heaven. At last, we had the correct paperwork. We had Guatemalan currency. We knew the city of Tapachula and the road to the border. It seemed nothing could stop this, our third attempt to leave the country.

Back at the border, we waved once more at our friends in the black market. We rolled past them and parked our bikes to check in with Mexican immigration. They quickly cleared us and we rode across a bridge into Guatemala.

I suppose it would be more accurate to say that we left Mexico and entered a state of limbo between countries. We found ourselves in a dirty little border town, riding slowly through chaotic pedestrian traffic. Out of the masses some guy waved us down and demanded a toll for something, possibly the bridge. Clearly, the man had the authority to do so; he owned a laminated badge.

We idled through throngs of people while keeping our eyes open for some kind of official building or checkstop. I held the theory that any required stop would be unavoidable, or at least noticeable, but somehow we managed to ride right past the Guatemalan Immigration Office. We parked the bikes, gathered our paperwork and walked back down the crowded street in search of the office.

We could have simplified the search. Six or seven kids had been running after us since Mexico, offering to help us cross the border. These boys, called *tramitadores*, make their living by helping tourists cut through the red tape in exchange for *propina*, or loose change. It's a fair price to ask, especially considering our Mexican coins were suddenly useless; money-changers only accept bills. Still, Trevor and I stubbornly refused their help. Some people claim that *tramitadores* make border crossings faster but more expensive, by skimming money from bribes and paperwork fees. We told the boys we didn't need them and we wouldn't pay, but they kept scrambling for our attention and pointing alternately at themselves and the direction we should go. Eventually Trevor and I wore most of them down. All but two *tramitadores* left to find more willing customers.

We located the immigration office, filled out several forms, and collected more stamps in our passports before returning to our bikes. The bikes sat at another stop along the obstacle course in no man's land, a fumigation station disguised as a single-pad, open-air car wash. We paid a small fee for a guy wearing a ventilator, coveralls, gloves and rubber boots to spray our tires with some kind of chemical. Judging by the man's personal protective equipment, the solution may have contained traces of Ebola.

After the fumigation we rode another hundred metres to what looked like the official border. A rusty chain stretched across the road and provided the last line of defence against travellers entering Guatemala. We parked the bikes and went into the office to produce our paperwork yet again, where we learned we needed photocopies of every form and stamp that we had filled out or received.

By this time, our shirts clung heavily to our sweaty bodies. Most exposed flesh had collected a thin film of international grime that turned our skin dark brown. My hair hung down into my eyes and stuck to the back of my neck. Trevor and I no longer refused assistance from the two remaining *tramitadores*, but wearily followed them back into the crowded streets to find a copy shop, returning with a stack of paper that could choke a camel.

We received more forms and paid more fees. Our passports, already heavy with stickers and stamps, disappeared behind the window of the customs office while we left to pay for our tourist visas at another window in another building. Our *tramitadores*, seeing my frustration growing at an unsustainable pace, uttered words of reassurance in broken English.

"Okay, okay," they said.

Finally we got our passports back and someone signed us into a huge

Guatemalan guestbook. Two men lowered the chain into a groove worn in the asphalt and we rolled triumphantly into another country.

"We're in GUATEMALA!" Trevor yelled over the noise of the engines as we rode side by side.

"And we RODE here!" I yelled back.

It had been a slow, frustrating day. Hours of lineups and wasted riding had left us merely 40 kilometres from where we'd started. It was far later than we would have liked and I was anxious to put some highway behind us. Trevor was in no hurry. For some reason he still had pesos he needed to convert. I waited impatiently while he stopped to buy more quetzals. Then we rode for a few minutes and Trevor pulled over to change into pants. (We usually rode in long pants for safety, but we'd both worn shorts that day, anticipating hours of uncomfortable heat at the border.)

We'd had nothing to eat during our crossing, so I grabbed a quick snack and a long drink of water while Trevor changed. I hopped back in the saddle, eager to ride, but Trevor was still digging in his pack looking for something to eat. It nearly drove me nuts the way the pack sort of exploded whenever he touched it. As he struggled to create order from chaos, I examined the maps.

Our destination was a city in the highlands called Quetzaltenango. Most people refer to the city by its traditional Mayan name, Xelajú or Xela for short. We had two options for reaching the city from our location. We could follow the direct path that wound through the mountains or the circuitous route through the flatlands to the south. We chose the southern route, reasoning that the flat, straight road would be faster than the short, winding one.

The highway, unobstructed by villages, allowed us to average nearly 100 kilometres per hour. My cheeks pressed firmly against the soft padding of my helmet owing to the enormous grin on my face. We'd merely crossed a political line at the frontier, a line on a piece of paper or a chain on the road; even so, every tree, every turn in the highway, every road sign and every person we passed seemed distinctly Guatemalan. Suddenly the experience was fresh and exciting again and I couldn't wait to explore this country further.

In Mexico we had given up hope of reaching Xela by nightfall, but we'd moved so swiftly since then that we decided to push on. We turned north and began climbing into the mountains. Xela is nestled in a high valley approximately 2,400 metres (8,000 feet) above sea level. It cooled rapidly and started to rain as we gained elevation.

We pulled over to put on rain gear. I put my rain suit on and had a snack before I looked over at Trevor. He was struggling with his rain pants and jacket, not to mention the shrapnel of miscellaneous items strewn about his bike from unpacking. I sat on my bike and hung my head as the rain trickled down my back.

"I've never ridden in the rain," said Trevor.

And you may never have to at this rate, I thought as I watched him fight to close and secure his pack.

We rolled into Xela at dusk and stumbled upon a really nice room in a clean, cheap hotel. The room even had a TV. After a long, stressful day, it hardly mattered that the only viewing choices in English were movies starring Patrick Swayze or Sandra Bullock.

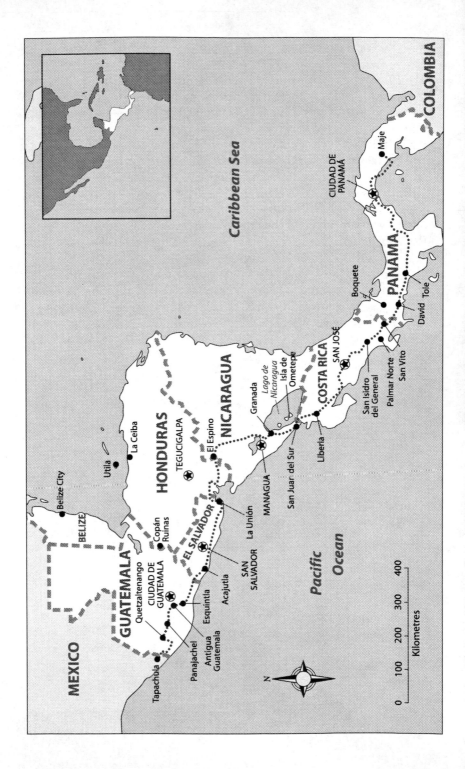

PART

2

November 15

Guatemala is renowned for its Spanish schools and Xela has become a popular place for budget travellers to study the language. I needed to learn how to say "I am hot" instead of "I am horny," so we set off to find a Spanish school immediately after breakfast.

We'd researched schools on the Internet before leaving Mexico and had a short list of prospective candidates. I liked the first school we saw, partly due to the receptionist. She had caramel skin and long brown hair. She greeted us enthusiastically with fluent English, remembering our names from e-mails we had sent while in San Cristóbal.

The facilities made a positive impression on me, as well. Bright, colourful handprints from hundreds of former students decorated the clean white walls of the foyer. A wooden staircase led up to cozy classrooms and a modest student lounge.

The school provided five hours of one-on-one instruction per day with a qualified teacher, and room and board with a local family, all for 125 dollars US per week. I wanted to sign up right then, but we left to check out a few other schools on our list before making a decision.

In the end, we found no school had outstanding advantages or disadvantages. I suggested we return to the first school with the colourful handprints and sign up. Trevor remained silent.

There's something you should know about Trevor. His method of expressing dissatisfaction or uncertainty is to gap out, go completely unresponsive. This comatose state often left me searching for some kind of *Ctrl + Alt + Del* for his brain, but I never found it. Suddenly he would snap back to attention, saying, "My brain isn't functioning today," or "My brain isn't working right now." Then he'd laugh as though that were an absurd exaggeration. If I had a nickel for every time he made references to insufficient cognitive ability, I could have paid for two weeks of Spanish classes.

I suppose I'm being hard on Trevor. After all, it had become very apparent to me that he and I occupied opposite ends of the patience spectrum. I have the attention span of a goldfish. I get bored easily and I'm apt to jump into situations without fully considering the consequences. I tried telling myself that Trevor's methods had merit – he's never been airlifted off a mountain by the Austrian military, for example – but most times his methods precluded action, and it was a source of constant frustration for me.

And so we found ourselves back at the first school. I had nearly finished filling out the application while Trevor continued to stare at the receptionist, considering all manner of pros and cons. I chatted briefly with another student in the lobby before Trevor finally put pen to paper.

That night, we attended a professional football game with some other students. The highly popular Xela Super Chivos faced a close rival and the small stadium brimmed with excitable spectators. The scene reminded me of my first time scuba diving in the sense that I had entered an entirely other world of sensory overload. Unlike diving, however, this time my sense of smell got in on the action. Strange aromatic combinations of smoke, sausage, gunpowder, fresh fruit, rotting meat, coffee, sweat and blood cycled through the air like an olfactory kaleidoscope.

Being from North America, where everything is pre-manufactured or processed beyond view of the consumer, it seemed strange to see vendors preparing snacks on the concrete bleachers, roasting sausages or boiling tea over coal-fired grills. The open flame remained unattended amongst the crowd as the vendor wandered the aisles, selling her product.

Young boys patrolled the stadium with wooden shoeshine boxes carried over their shoulders with leather straps. With their tattered dress shirts and pants, many of them resembled old men, and some even hobbled as if the weariness of old age had claimed them prematurely. Their faces and hands were black with polish and the dirty baseball caps they wore sat crookedly on their heads.

Other boys walked the aisle with boxes of candy and cigarettes, but the girls seemed mostly restricted to selling drinks. One particularly pretty girl did especially well with her business. She was slender with black hair, dressed in tight jeans and a lacy white blouse with open shoulders. Almost everyone turned his head to watch her as she walked by, returning his attention to the game only when she had passed. Obviously conscious of the lustful eyes upon her, she tolerated the whistles and catcalls as long as she could make a sale. She never smiled.

Other women selling drinks carried colourful wraps on their backs stuffed with terror-stricken children. The fear in their faces was justifiable. Whenever someone scored a goal, the raucous crowd pressed against the chain-link fence surrounding the field as if involved in a prison riot.

Bottle rockets whistled through the crowd and Trevor took one off the shoulder. The rocket fell to the ground and exploded with an impressive concussion. Smoke bombs went off at random intervals, stinging our eyes. Airhorns and trumpets blew, drums pounded and the crowd sang through the entire game. The home team scored the winning goal in the last minute and the mob rushed the fence in ecstasy.

That night represents the best five dollars I've ever spent. Exhausted, I returned to the hotel and watched the only thing on TV: *Roadhouse*, starring Patrick Swayze.

November 16

We met and moved in with our host families. Trevor and I had the option of staying with the same family, but we never even considered it.

My accommodation turned out to be with a family of four in a single-storey building made of brick and plaster on the corner of two streets.

From the street, it appeared as if each house or shop were part of one solid structure spanning a whole block, each building running into the next and defined only by differing heights or colours. Most buildings had clay tile roofs, and this one was no exception. It had six rooms and a central courtyard, but it was by no means spacious. The largest room opened onto a side street and provided storage for our motorbikes and the family's meagre possessions.

Two bedrooms housed two student boarders, including myself. The furnishings in my room consisted of two lumpy beds, one wooden chair, a candle, a table and a bare light bulb that hung on a long cord from the ceiling. The window opened onto the narrow side street and provided a much better view with the wooden shutters closed.

The entire host family lived and slept in a small room adjoining the tiny kitchen. The only other room housed half a dozen tables with plastic tablecloths and served as a rudimentary restaurant that opened onto the main street.

My host mother, Rosaria, took care of her infant daughter and diligently tended the restaurant, but during my two-week stay I only saw her serve one customer. The rest of the business came from me and my fellow students, who dutifully depleted stocks of beer after hours, merely as an act of selfless charity to help a family in need.

Rudy, the man of the house, did little else but sit around watching his wife work. He loved to talk, and conversing with him in Spanish provided great learning opportunities – but the real tutor was Pablo.

Just six years old, Pablo became fast friends with me as we studied some of the same things in school. In the evenings we did our homework together. I helped him with simple math, and he taught me how to conjugate verbs.

After weeks of constant movement, it felt strange to have a routine. Each day I spent five hours practising how to say, "*No comprendo*" while my teacher reached heights of boredom I hitherto thought only attainable in theory. I tried to lighten the mood by learning phrases like, "If you don't cancel your signal light, I'll punch you in the back of the head." But mostly I just amused myself, and even that became difficult.

I ate simple meals with my host family, occasionally interrupting conversation with grammatically incorrect comments on non-related topics, much the same way I converse in English. In the afternoon I studied vocabulary with fellow students at what may be the best coffee shop in Central America.

Bavaria's is a quiet little place, staffed by local women wearing colourful dresses. The baristas sit on a step, sorting green coffee beans on their laps. The beans are roasted and ground at the shop, and transformed into dark coffee with a creamy froth the colour of honey and cinnamon, served in an elegant white cup on a saucer with two white sugar cookies.

Our study and social group included five people. Of course, there was Trevor. The best efforts of Spanish speakers to pronounce his name would always be "Tree-bol," and Tree-bol he became. For similar reasons, I became "Jeremias" with a soft "J" as in jalapeño. Jeremias had a dignified ring and I happily adopted the moniker for the remainder of the trip.

Jordan, a tall, dark-haired kid from Australia, had a quick wit and quicker smile. He traveled with Ohad, a non-religious Jew and amateur philosopher with a thick black beard and hair. Ohad seemed well-educated, a real critical thinker.

The final member of our group was also named Trevor, and – to avoid confusion – became "*Otra* Tree-bol" (Other Trevor), or "*Otra*" for short. Unless I miss my guess, I detected flirtatious tension between us. (I should mention that *Otra* was a girl. I should also mention that my default assumption is that every girl is attracted to me.) *Otra* had short, dark hair and wore glasses. Occasionally she wore a low-cut shirt revealing a large tattoo of a dragonfly across her chest.

November 20

The darkened bar pulsed with dim lights and sensual energy. Bodies intertwined, flowing into one another like milk and honey to the steady throb of a salsa beat. I couldn't have been more conspicuous standing there had I been wearing a black hat and suspenders, carrying a pitchfork and having arrived in a horse-drawn buggy with a reflective orange triangle.

I'm a Mennonite. I have to face that fact. It means that I have some baggage in life that I must carry, but I have my dignity to carry as well. As a Mennonite, I cannot pronounce "lunch," "thrilled," or any word that contains vowels, really. More to the point, I cannot dance. I can dig. I can ride a horse and say things like "prepare to meet thy doom, English" and mean it.

"Let's go salsa dancing," they said.

"It'll be fun," they said.

My inner voice screamed words of reason – good, true words that rang with divine wisdom, but I would not heed them. Oh, that the images burned into my eyes would relent and allow me a moment of peace, but alas, they will not. Debauchery has a new name – I dub thee *salsa*.

November 22

I hate hiking. I think it's dangerous and I've sustained enough serious injuries to prove it. Whatever possessed me to include a hiking pole in my otherwise minimalistic equipment is beyond me. Perhaps my decision to climb a volcano served merely to justify bringing the stupid pole from Canada. Whatever the reason, I found myself in the back of a little white pickup truck jolting towards the trailhead in the chilly blackness of pre-dawn with Ohad, Trevor, a few other students and the pole.

We parked the truck as the sun came up, and began walking. The trail wound through lush fields tended by farmers in the morning mist before turning steeply up the muddy slope of an active volcano called Santa Maria.

The front side of Santa Maria, the side that faces Xela, remains forested and uniformly conical, but looking down from the summit, one can see on the flank evidence of a massive eruption that occurred in 1902. It appears as if a third of the dome has sloughed off, raking the forest from top to bottom and leaving a tortured scar of washed-out grey. I followed the path of the slide with my eyes until about halfway down, where I could see a mound of rocky debris, a lava dome named Santiaguito.

Santiaguito first appeared in 1922 and remains regularly active. It erupted shortly after we reached the summit of Santa Maria, sending a thick column of gas and ash into the air. The plume blossomed, rising from beneath us until we had to look up to see its upper limits. Far below, we could see large rocks tumbling down the slope, disappearing from view just as the faint sound of their retreat reached our ears. Shortly after the eruption, the clouds closed in below us like a thick curtain between us and Santiaguito, effectively ending the show. Above, the sky remained brilliantly clear except for fading billows of the eruption column. We lay in the sun for a long time before heading back down.

November 23

While studying in a park near my house, I noticed an impossibly beautiful girl with dark hair and alabaster skin sitting on a bench across from me. She brushed a lock of hair from her face and tucked it behind her ear while she sat reading. I couldn't take my eyes from her. I think Trevor may have sat down beside me and said something, but I don't know. All I knew was that if I didn't talk to this girl I would always wish I had.

She remained absorbed in her book until I stood right beside her, intrusively blocking her sun. When she looked up I introduced myself, quivering with nervous excitement. I wanted to place my hand on my chest to steady my heart, but reached out to shake her hand instead. The girl spoke with a German accent and invited me to sit. We talked for a while, but I decided to cut the conversation short; with all the adrenaline pumping through me I could only just make out my own words, and the probability of me saying something inexplicably weird increased every second.

As luck would have it, I had two activities planned for the day. I intended to visit a cemetery with the usual bunch of people from school, and I planned to see my favourite movie, *Bottle Rocket*, that night in a nearby theatre. While the former event might have seemed creepy and strange, the latter typified a first date experience in most western civilizations and might provide the perfect opportunity to get to know the girl. I stood up and swallowed hard before I could muster the courage to ask her out. "You wanna go to a cemetery?" I stammered. I should have punched myself in the face as hard as I could right then and there.

"Um, which one?" she asked.

"I don't know."

To make things simple, I told her to meet me at that very spot in two hours if she intended to come along. She said she might. She said it in such a way that meant I would never see her on that bench for the rest of my stay in Guatemala, and I never did.

November 24

Through the grimy windows of our crowded bus, I stared at the blur of fields divided by walls of rock as we wound our way through a river valley on the way to Zunil. Trevor and I, along with several other students from our school, got off at the little village that clung to the side of a steep hill and played host to San Simón. San Simón, also known as Maximón, is an idol representing an awkward blend of Mayan and Catholic religions. Highly revered by locals, Maximón is considered a reincarnation of Mam, a Mayan god, and a deification of Pedro de Alvarado, the Spanish conquistador responsible for the conversion of many Mayans to Catholicism. In Zunil, as in every village that boasts an effigy of the unauthorized saint, the idol has no permanent dwelling place. On the first day of every November, Maximón gets moved amidst pomp and circumstance to a different house, where worshipers are then charged an admission to see him.

While most of my fellow students, unwilling to pay, milled around the dusty yard philosophising about money and god, I paid the small fee and entered the sanctuary. Nothing could have prepared me for what I saw.

It took my eyes several moments to adjust as I stepped out of the bright sunlight into the dark room. The only sources of light came from the open door, a small window and dozens of prayer candles. The candles, along with their plastic holders, melted into colourful puddles on the dirt floor, saturating the air with smoke that reeked of burning plastic.

I rubbed my eyes. Through a nearly palpable haze, I could see him at the front of the room. Maximón was a life-sized mannequin draped in colourful blankets and seated with impeccable posture on a high-backed wooden chair. He wore a cowboy hat and boots, leather gloves, a wide purple tie with a Windsor knot, and a pair of gaudy aviator sunglasses. The glasses, though certainly large, could not mask the comical expression of shock on his face. His features simultaneously reminded me of Howdy Doody and Michael Jackson.

I sat quietly on a wooden bench at the back of the room, observing the spectacle. Worshippers brought offerings of cigarettes, perfume and rum to Maximón, who always appeared surprised by their generosity. To offer drinks, people gently tipped his chair back and poured the liquid into his mouth, catching the alcoholic discharge from the back of his head in a plastic basin.

As soon as Maximón finished drinking, worshippers placed a lit cigarette in his mouth. This guy could party. People prayed to him, kissed him and patted him on the back with great reverence. Women knelt at his side, others placed money in his pockets and children touched him tenderly.

The faithful came and went, but two people remained with Maximón at all times. An elderly man and woman filled the gaps between worshippers by keeping cigarettes lit in his mouth and praying without ceasing. They clearly adored him.

At first I thought devotion to such a comical-looking puppet was the funniest thing I had ever seen. The longer I stayed, the more it seemed the saddest thing I had seen.

"It makes more sense praying to a god you can't see," observed Ohad, who had quietly slipped in beside me. He had an interesting way of summing up profound thoughts with simple statements.

We visited an ornate Catholic church after leaving the sanctuary of Maximón. Hundreds of prayer candles burned at the feet of a carved image of Jesus.

"These people just spend more money on their idols," Ohad remarked.

November 27

After two intense weeks of Spanish classes, I could say *"No entiendo,"* (I don't understand) and *"No comprendo"* (I don't understand) with a perfectly clean accent. I learned other phrases as well, such as "*Yo tengo una pregunta.*" (I have a question.) I could then ask my simple question and follow it up with "*No entiendo*" once I heard the response.

And so, my time in Guatemala drew to a close. I had one more day of classes, which meant another five hours of saying "*No comprendo*" before loading up my bike and hitting the road. I looked forward to the sound of a roaring engine instead of the roar of laughter from Spanish speakers when, meaning to say "I love the mountains," I actually said "I love prostitutes."

November 27

After supper I packed most of my stuff and loaded my bike. The process of packing, which had become routine in the past several weeks, suddenly felt difficult and inefficient.

Pablo came into my room and moped around while I packed. He sat down on my bed and remained silent until I spoke.

"How are you doing, Pablo?" I asked.

"Fine," he replied, but he kept his eyes on the floor.

"Really? You look sad."

Pablo's eyes remained fixed on the floor and he said nothing.

"Are you sad?" I asked.

Pablo nodded. He was trying to be brave, and doing a good job for such a small boy. I stopped packing and sat down on the bed.

"Why are you sad, Pablo?" I pressed. He waited a long time to answer.

"Because…" Pablo trailed off. When he continued his voice trembled and faltered in the end, "Because you're leaving!"

That nearly broke my heart. In two weeks we had developed a real friendship. I occasionally accepted his frequent invitations to watch cartoons in his cramped living quarters. I did homework with him in the evenings, and asked him to tell me about his day at school. I taught him some English and let him play on my motorbike. That's all it takes for a young boy to grow attached to someone. Then again, that's all it took for me to grow attached to him.

Pablo never cried, though I could tell that he had to fight the urge with all his strength. When he left my room, I imagine he found comfort in the arms of his mother. Or perhaps he tried to hide his sorrow from her as he had tried to hide it from me. All I know is, that night, in that house, two brave men choked back the urge to cry.

November 28

Following a two-week break, Trevor and I felt refreshed and eager to ride. We still irritated each other, but our partnership had grown stronger and we even had some goals: we would at least try to ride to Panama.

We finished packing and rode into the streets of Xela, streets we knew like the backs of our hands. Within five minutes we got lost. We circled by known landmarks along familiar streets and past many friends, including Ohad, Jordan, Rudy and *Otra*. Their enthusiasm at seeing us waned with each lap of our misguided farewell tour until they eventually pretended not to see us, graciously saving us further embarrassment.

When we finally broke the code and escaped the city, Trevor executed a celebratory motorcycle crash by grabbing his front brake while cornering on gravel.

"Did you see that?" he asked in astonishment. How could I have missed it? He'd crashed about six feet in front of me.

Trevor lifted his machine and we hit the highway, passing people and making fleeting eye contact with many as we sped by. You've probably experienced this in a car. You pass someone on the road and, for one reason or another, you lock eyes for just a moment. Well, it happens all the time on a motorcycle. For one instant, you establish a connection, if only a superficial one; the connection is without context and quickly lost. The people you see through the helmet visor become like snapshots on a View-Master image reel.

Load the reel. Pull the handle. Click.

An old man with creased, leather skin wearing a straw cowboy hat and a thick, woollen skirt like a drab kilt.

Click.

An optimistic-looking young man, a vendor on the shoulder displaying rows of deer intricately woven from branches or straw.

Click.

Naked children playing near a brick shack, a shack perched danger-ously alongside a steep, earthen bank.

Click.

An old woman in bright colours carrying a basket of bread.

Is the old man lonely? Does the vendor sell enough to feed his family? Would the children survive the next heavy rain? Is the old woman happy? The images never tell; they only underscore a certain sense of isolation as you slip by, leaving the people behind and the questions unanswered.

Our bikes coughed in the thin air, labouring to maintain momen-tum over high plains and mountain passes. We rode higher than the tree line of any jagged Canadian mountain, but the rolling and smooth Guatemalan highlands lay beneath a quilt of cornfields with thick patches of trees.

We turned off the main road, finally descending into a volcanic basin towards Panajachel on the shore of Lago de Atitlán, a caldera. The smooth, narrow road twisted its way deeper into a ring of dark green peaks that cradled the sparkling water of the lake like God's fingerbowl.

As I settled into my room in Panajachel, a wave of emotion washed over me. *Otra* had given me a bag of cookies when she said goodbye; I sat on my bed eating them and missing her.

But it was more than that. Before arriving in Xela, Trevor and I had relocated every other day, seldom staying in one place long enough to unpack. When we got to Xela, we'd lost our momentum. We established routines. We found favourite coffee shops. We made friends.

When it came time to leave, it felt like the start of another trip, a trip I hadn't prepared for. I was anxious to go, but sad at the same time. I guess the emotional dissonance finally caught up to me when I sat on my bed and quietly reflected on the way the cookie crumbles.

November 29

Just for fun, Trevor and I boarded a passenger boat bound for a vil-lage on the other side of the lake, San Pedro. The little vessel rose and fell gently on rather large waves.

At San Pedro, a steep cobblestone road led us away from the dock and we bumped into some friends from Xela, Connie and Ian. Together we explored the dirt roads and narrow paths lined with banana trees and coffee plants. Cute little girls with an apparent knack for market analysis wandered the streets selling handmade bracelets, necklaces and glass marijuana pipes. As evening approached we returned to the dock and caught a boat back to Panajachel.

The gentle swells that had carried our little ship to San Pedro had become downright menacing, pitching and rolling the boat, dipping its gunwales dangerously close to the choppy water. In a desperate attempt to keep the boat from swamping, passengers rolled down canvas walls over a wooden frame, but the leaky canopy provided all the help of a blindfold on a man before a firing squad. As we drew farther away from land and the lake became more turbulent, the passengers' nervous laughter turned to nervous silence. The ride would have been a virtual hell on earth for anyone with the slightest fear of water.

I should mention Ian's mortal fear of water. When all 20 passengers suddenly reached for their lifejackets, Ian – who had donned his before taking a seat in the boat – clung to the gunwales with ashen fingers and a dire expression on his face.

As for me, I decided to remain calm until our young captain showed sign of fear, but he never did. With a slight smile, he pressed into the heavy spray, his pink poncho flapping about his neck like a windsock. I never even put my lifejacket on.

We went for drinks that evening in Panajachel. Ian wanted to celebrate the precious gift of life and one more fragile day on the planet. I merely wanted to celebrate beer.

November 30

Trevor and I left the bustling street markets and cool lakefront setting of Panajachel and headed for Antigua. We rode up the same switchbacked road we'd come in on and stopped to take some photos looking down on Lago de Atitlán. Other than that, the rest of the ride is completely lost in my memory, until the end.

As usual, I rode in front and confidently led us past our destination on obscure roads to a town that didn't exist on our maps. We backtracked to Antigua following an emotionally heated, illogical debate in which we both lost our tempers over issues that we never discussed.

Perhaps my mind was still on the argument, or perhaps I was just tired after another day of riding; whatever the reason, I failed to notice a patch of sand on a tight corner in the road. My heart jumped into my throat when my tires started to slide and I instinctively put my foot down to arrest the fall, but at 60 kilometres per hour, slapping your foot to pavement is seldom a good idea. In less than a second, many thoughts flashed through my panicked mind – thoughts like "I should have stretched this morning," and "I wonder when I'll reach the physical limit of the human hip joint's range of motion... oh! There it is!"

Anyone with an understanding of Newton's Laws of Motion can imagine what happened. My foot stopped momentarily. The bike kept going. My foot (being attached to my leg) struggled to catch up with rest of me, which had already traveled some distance. The ensuing arcing motion of my leg is analogous to an elite fastball pitcher executing a blinding windmill pitch.

Somehow I managed to maintain control. My foot stung and my leg ached for several minutes as painful reminders that an accident could happen at any moment. Trevor and I had been fortunate so far, and we had begun taking safety for granted. As we arrived in Antigua, we both looked at each other and shook our heads. No words necessary.

We found a nice room close to the main square in Antigua, but the matriarch of the hostel would only allow one motorbike in her living room. That seemed unreasonable and we pleaded with her in choppy Spanish to reconsider. Well, I pleaded. Trevor hopped around wearing an incredulous expression, miming exactly how we could position the bikes and saying, "Oooo. Oooo? Oo." Judging from his intonation and corresponding hand signals, one got the impression that Trevor truly believed these utterances conveyed a specific message. However, even I, well aware of the desired outcome, could not decipher their meaning. Regardless, the landlady allowed us poor, inarticulate souls to bring both bikes inside for an additional fee.

The old lady kept several colourful birds in the landing, and one insane squirrel. Squirrels are not meant for cages. All day the squirrel sat and waited for death, motionless, its tail pressed against its back and curling up over its head. I watched it with pity for some time, examining the critter for any sign of hope or awareness in its glassy eyes.

What thoughts lurked behind those eyes? Do squirrels pray? Did this one pray for mercy and deliverance to tiny gods? Or did it believe the old woman was god, worshipping her for providing food and blaming itself for the cage? Perhaps it thought of me as god – merciful, maybe, but powerless.

I wanted to reach into the cage and save the squirrel from its little hell. I wanted to buy it from the old lady and set it free, but I knew better. Even if I left the cage door open for weeks, or removed an entire wall from the wire enclosure, it would make little difference. The animal would undoubtedly remain on its perch, unable or unwilling to accept its freedom. Anyway, the thing probably never considered god or any world outside of its prison; it was just a stupid squirrel.

I sighed heavily and looked away.

To understand why the sight bothered me, picture the same squirrel huddled in front of a tiny television tuned to the *National Geographic* Channel. I could relate. Only my cage had manifested itself as an intangible tripod of injury, boredom and loneliness. Of course, the tripod had faded into a bad memory now. My motorbike had delivered me from the worst of my depression. My half-baked plan seemed to be working, just not as well as I had hoped.

You see, as trustworthy and liberating as it was, the bike could not touch my loneliness. I still felt hollow. What's worse, the machine seemed to guide me into situations that magnified flaws in my character: impatience, anger, resentment, self-absorption. No mere blemishes, but deep-seated, ugly traits of character that threatened to destroy relationships with those I loved. Leave it to me to turn a little vacation into a page torn from the awkward motorcycle version of Joseph Conrad's *Heart of Darkness*.

I painfully searched my memory. Had I been a victim of Susan's infidelity, or an unwitting conspirator? Was Trevor irritating, or was I irritable? In both cases, almost certainly it was a bit of both.

"Is that thing real?" asked Trevor, glancing at the squirrel as he approached. I looked at the squirrel and nodded.

"Let's grab something to eat," he said and we left the building, thus sparing me any further introspection.

Antigua is a well preserved colonial city with domes and archways that reminded me of Europe. Blocky buildings stained with white trim and most of nature's subtler colours line the streets. Iron bars guard every window and clay tile roofs cap most buildings. We ambled along cobblestone roads to a nearby park with a tall fountain where we bumped into Connie and Ian.

It seems an odd coincidence, meeting people you know in a large city in a foreign country, but it happens all the time. We told them about our short, pleasant motorcycle ride, and they told us about their long, uncomfortable chicken bus journey.

Chicken busses are found throughout Latin America. When a school bus in North America no longer meets emissions requirements, they ship it south where it lives out the remainder of its days at the hands of a maniacal driver. Most busses get plastered with a gaudy paint scheme and, if the owner can afford it, enough chrome and coloured lights to shame any self-respecting disco-ball. Chicken busses provide cheap, unsafe, unreliable transportation for tourists, locals and domestic animals.

December 2

We set out early for El Salvador, turning our backs on hazy mountains and riding towards the Pacific Ocean on a flat highway. When we stopped to check our maps near Esquintla, we noticed a plume of smoke rising from a distant peak. We watched the eruption in silence for a few moments before turning east towards the border. Our *tramitadore,* Freddie, suggested we buy a transit permit to Costa Rica to save time and money, a decision we would later regret. The whole afternoon became a blur of lines, forms, computer malfunctions, fees and intolerable heat. It took us from 11:30 a.m. to 4:30 p.m. to cross into El Salvador.

We raced the setting sun to a seaside town just off the main highway called Acajutla. A young man on a bicycle, who wanted nothing in return for his help, led us to a nearly vacant hotel by the ocean. The operators stared at us in utter disbelief for a few moments before they remembered what to do with paying customers. We paid six dollars each for our own insect-infested rooms, where we cooked supper.

I inherited a cast-iron stomach and appreciation for simple food from my Grandpa. I never tire of a repetitive menu, a necessity given that I am a culinary idiot. Whenever Trevor asked what I felt like eating, and I mean every time, I'd nonchalantly say "How about rice and eggs?"

The predictability of my response began to make Trevor visibly upset, forcing me to mix it up a bit. Sometimes, when asked what I wanted for supper, I'd furrow my brow and look down. It appeared to Trevor as if I was thinking of food ideas, but in my mind I was just dancing around the room, clapping my hands and chanting, "Rice and eggs! Rice and eggs! Rice and eggs!"

I could feel the tension growing in the room as Trevor waited for me to speak. I imagined him thinking, "Don't say rice and eggs. Don't say rice and eggs. Don't say rice and eggs." When I could bear the silence no longer, I'd look up as though I'd just had an idea and say, "How about," (pause for dramatic effect) "rice and eggs?"

The problem was one of perspective. Trevor looked at his plate and saw bland, unimaginative food barely containing the basic ingredients to sustain life. I looked at my plate and saw a veritable cornucopia of flavour and blessed nutrients. Also, it was cheap and easy to make on our little gasoline camping stove. No doubt the whole cooking thing annoyed Trevor as much as his signal light annoyed me, but at least monotonous dinners wouldn't cause a horrible traffic accident.

Once again, Trevor asked what I wanted for supper – I can't imagine why. I furrowed my brow and looked down as if in thought.

After a fantastic supper of rice and eggs, we relaxed on the patio and enjoyed several wonderfully cold malt beverages under a sparkling night sky. The warm breeze and rhythmic sound of the ocean fostered a melancholy mood. I became homesick and lonely, suddenly daunted by the journey ahead.

I looked over at Trevor, scribbling thoughtfully in his journal at the next table.

"Hey Trev," I interrupted.

Trevor looked up and grabbed his beer.

"Do you think we'll actually make it to Panama?" I said.

"Of course. Why wouldn't we?" Trevor took a swig and looked out at the ocean before turning back to his journal.

December 3

A warm wind snapped at my nylon jacket as we rode along El Salvador's majestic coastal highway. It was another perfect moment. I could see Trevor riding in front of me, silhouetted against the glistening Pacific, when suddenly, something eclipsed the sun. Slowly, deliberately, I turned my gaze to check my rear-view mirror and gasped at what I saw.

The frame of my mirror contained nothing but one enormous headlight of a transport truck that was riding my tail and closing the distance. *That guy's so close I can nearly touch his bumper,* I thought and, for reasons I can't explain, my body considered that a command.

I twisted around to face the truck, keeping my right hand steady on the throttle to maintain our delicate equilibrium. Resting my torso on the backpack strapped to my rear seat and reaching as far back as I could with my left arm, I extended my index finger. I could not touch the bumper, so (and this I really can't explain), I gently *rolled back the throttle.* The look of bewilderment and horror on the driver's face as he slammed on his brakes was very entertaining and I instantly had plenty of room.

It took us one long, hot day to cover 300 kilometres and cross the entire country of El Salvador. Trevor and I rolled into La Unión and rented two rooms in a cheap hotel. After some bike maintenance we went for a walk in search of food.

The sun set while we ate and the city suffered a massive power failure. On the way back, we practically had to grope our way in the direction of the hotel. When the lights began blinking on at random locations in the city, we found ourselves in a wet street market that smelled of rotten meat.

I couldn't believe my eyes. I cast a quick glance at Trevor to recalibrate my vision, and looked back at the girl. I hadn't imagined her.

She stood beneath the only functioning streetlight in an otherwise darkened alley as though the light, inspired by her beauty, had decided to illuminate her. Her red, strapless gown shimmered on her slender form as she brushed a wisp of silky black hair from her face with the back of a delicate hand. With the other hand, she held a lucky ice cream cone. She gently carved shallow grooves in the ice cream with the very tip of her tongue, occasionally catching a runaway drip with a deadly kiss before it could touch the soft skin of her fingers. Her tiara broke the light into a thousand pieces, scattering colourful glints to even the darkest corners of the filthy alley.

A drunken man urinated on the sidewalk only a few metres from her, possibly pissing the Spanish word for "juxtaposition" on the pavement. She took no notice and we kept walking.

We arrived at the hotel to discover that it sat across the street from the world's loudest outdoor disco. Of course, the obese landlady who sat smothering an unseen chair had failed to mention the disco, but readily admitted prior knowledge when asked how long the music would disturb our sleep: "*Toda la noche!*" (All night) she cackled, while fanning herself with a magazine.

It's difficult to overstate the volume of the bass-thumping techno music that blasted across the street. Windows rattled, the garbage can shook and the pencils on my nightstand hopped around like Mexican jumping beans. I didn't sleep, exactly. Rather, my mind retreated somewhere deep inside my head and manually shut down my senses, inducing a sort of coma.

December 4

Once more suffering from food poisoning, Trevor decided to visit a hospital. I'd suggested he take the broad range antibiotics we'd brought from home, but he wanted to see a doctor. When he came back he said the whole hospital visit had been a waste of time. Then he took his broad range antibiotics.

We got a late start because of the delay and arrived at the El Salvador border with Honduras at one in the afternoon. We idled through a sea of laminated badges, finally choosing a *tramitadore* with golden eye teeth, one bearing the inscription *J* and the other *T*. Assuredly, we would glide through the border with JT's help and he snapped his fingers to prove it.

Of course, JT had no way of knowing that our transit permits had expired and that we had unwittingly overstayed our legal welcome in El Salvador by a whole day. Trevor and I didn't know that either; consequently we each needed to pay 55 dollars US just to leave the country. With little help from JT, we stood in long lines and argued with many people about the fine.

After we had spent about four hours sweating in a gravel parking lot, a pair of unshaven men dressed in leather and denim thumped up to the border on an old, Russian motorcycle. They spoke no Spanish. They spoke no English. They only spoke Russian. They showed us a map of their travels, which covered most of the globe, and then they roared on to Honduras, leaving Trevor and me in the dusty parking lot.

In frustration, we barged into the actual customs office to talk to someone in charge. (Don't try that at the Canada-US border, by the way.) We implied that we had overstayed our permit because of Trevor's illness. Trevor produced a crumpled hospital receipt for the officer's review.

The officer sat at his desk and examined the receipt.

"When did you visit the hospital?" he asked. The receipt had no date on it.

"This morning," Trevor replied.

"Not yesterday?" said the official. He glanced at the mountain of paperwork we had accumulated in the past four hours.

"No. I was in the hospital this morning."

"That's too bad. If you were in the hospital yesterday, that would change everything. You could just go."

We said nothing.

"Now," he continued, "when did you go to the hospital?"

"Right. I was in the hospital yesterday," said Trevor.

The officer smiled and quickly wrote yesterday's date on the receipt. He showed the receipt to his staff, yelling at them for their error and pointing to the date he had just written. The mountain of paperwork vanished and we left without paying any fines.

Exhausted, we ditched JT and rode into the night towards Honduras, but he hitched a ride with a trucker and caught up to us shortly after we arrived. He continued snapping his fingers in Honduras, but remained ineffective.

Trevor and I navigated innumerable queues with the jittery resignation of cattle in a slaughterhouse. Just as the physical and mental fatigue reached nearly unbearable levels, a lady prepared to stamp our passports, clearing us for entry into Honduras.

"Once I stamp these," she said, "you have six hours to make it to Nicaragua."

We looked at her in stunned silence. Apparently the transit papers we had purchased when leaving Guatemala, the same permits that limited us to 24 hours in El Salvador, only allowed us six hours in Honduras and something like 16 hours in Nicaragua.

"But it's dark out," we pleaded.

The lady handed us an unsympathetic stare.

"It's dangerous to ride at night," we added.

"No, it's not," she said.

"Yes, it is."

"No, it's not."

Meanwhile, the Russians we'd met earlier rode past the office and threw a friendly wave as they continued into the night. That didn't strengthen our position, but we were allowed to finish the paperwork in the morning. The clock would start ticking when the stamp hit our passports.

That left us with just one more person to yell at before bed: JT. He wanted his money.

"We had a deal. We would pay you when we made it into Honduras," I said. "We're not in Honduras, yet."

Still, for his time, I gave JT the price we originally agreed upon. He became furious and demanded more, arguing that he had given us an entire day.

"Yeah, an entire *useless* day," I said.

I kept arguing with him while Trevor left to attend to the bikes. JT pointed to some of his friends and then threatened to kill us in our sleep. At least, that's what I heard. Then again, it was late, my Spanish was poor and I was tired. Regardless, Trevor and I made an effort to avoid detection as we looked for a hotel.

We ended up in the most appalling room I have ever spent the night in, and this is coming from a man who considers aiming at stains in the toilet bowl while taking a pee to be light housework. I had to work up courage to use the toilet, and using the shower was simply out of the question. I slept on the bed only because it offered a slightly better alternative than the concrete floor, which crawled with insect and reptilian life.

Our evening meal, purchased from a nearby gas station, consisted of Pepsi, chocolate, Pringles and wieners in a can. After the day we had endured, the meal seemed better than any Christmas dinner I've ever had at Grandma's house.

December 5

Still covered in sweat and filth from the day before and additional filth collected during the night, we headed back into the fray to complete our paperwork. We spent several hours standing in line and shouting at people before an official finally stamped our passports with dramatic flair.

"Finished," he declared.

"No more?" we asked for clarification.

"No more," he said confidently.

"So, we can go to Nicaragua now?"

"Nicaragua, Costa Rica, Panama, *todo el mundo*," he assured us.

Our papers only allowed us six hours to cross Honduras and enter Nicaragua, but that was okay – after all the delays and frustration, we were eager to ride. We rode one happy kilometre before a guy on the road flagged us down. Not a guy in uniform, mind you. Not even a guy with a gun, or a whistle or a badge – just a guy, a kid, actually.

"You need to get your papers stamped," said the kid.

"Where?" I asked. The kid pointed. Three men lounged around a large desk at the side of the road under the shade of a tree.

"You're kidding," I said.

Not only did we need more stamps on our papers, but we needed photocopies of everything. As the concept of conveniently located copy machines has yet to occur to anyone in Central America, we hired the kid who had flagged us down to get copies from the nearest machine. He hopped on his bicycle and raced back to the border where we'd begun the day.

What a ridiculous system. For the remainder of the day I kept wondering if we would be stopped and told, "Okay. This is really, really, honestly, no kidding, absolutely the last thing you have to do before entering Honduras, I promise."

I had a few moments, however, when my thoughts shifted from the frustrations of border crossings to the urgency of survival. While riding through a gently undulating landscape of fields along a two-way road, an oncoming truck edged into my lane to see if it was safe to pass. He must have seen me on my little motorcycle and decided that, yes, it was indeed safe for him to pass. At least he had the courtesy to flash his lights, giving me the requisite heads up to slam on my brakes and swerve onto the tiny shoulder. I braced myself against a turbulent blast of abrasive air as the truck thundered by, mere centimetres away. I believe the trucker actually waved at me. Trevor waved back, though not with his entire hand.

The only other thing I remember about the short, six-hour ride through Honduras is seeing one perfect tree. It stood alone. Rooted in a rolling carpet of green, a dark spreading tree adorned with brilliant pink flowers.

With the help of a previously untapped resource, the bribe, we entered Nicaragua with unprecedented ease. The transit permit that had caused so many problems in El Salvador and Honduras disappeared, along with our stress.

"We're in Nicaragua!" I said as I climbed onto my bike.

"And we rode here!" Trevor replied.

Suddenly unencumbered by any concern regarding paperwork, borders or fines, the road into Nicaragua felt like the yellow brick road – magical. We rode side by side following freshly painted lines on smooth blacktop, standing on our foot pegs and leaning into the wind. Our fists pumped through the air in time to the telepathically audible beat of *Low Rider* while the lazy sun cast a golden light on pillowy hills of green.

In the spirit of quitting while ahead, we took refuge at a hotel before dusk. After settling into our room and hanging my mosquito net, I sauntered into the central courtyard of the hotel to check out its little zoo.

The curator obviously hated animals. Imprisoned monkeys suffered in cramped, filthy enclosures, lacking mental or physical stimuli. The ones strong enough to maintain some will to live had worn grooves in the floors of their cages from repetitive pacing, but most of the beasts sat gently rocking in a corner, or staring blankly through glassy eyes. The sight tarnished a magical day, but the worst was yet to come.

That night, Trevor and I awoke to terrible, primeval sounds. Tortured screams and slapping blows erupted from somewhere in the darkness. The insanity of the primate population must finally have reached an awful climax and the beasts were tearing their keeper to shreds, I thought.

Sadly, no.

By horrible degrees of increasing consciousness, I realized that the sounds emanated from the couple in the next room. The paper-thin walls did nothing to muffle the cries of drunken passion unfolding centimetres from where we slept. I will spare you and me any further description. Suffice it to say the pair had an insatiable collective libido, and they were nothing if not persistent... and disgusting. I'm really not talking about normal physical intimacy. I'm really not.

December 6

We settled into a hostel called the Bearded Monkey in Nicaragua's oldest colonial town, Granada. Founded in 1524, the town rests on the bank of Central America's largest lake, Lago de Nicaragua. Before the Panama Canal, engineers considered Lago de Nicaragua an option for linking the Atlantic and Pacific oceans.

Granada may have been old, but it had a youthful feel. Horse-drawn taxis shuttled tourists around a shady, central park nestled at the foot of a large white cathedral. Buildings of white, pink, yellow or blue ran together in typical Central American style. The city provided the perfect location to relax and recuperate. For two days, Trevor and I seldom ventured from our hammocks in the hostel courtyard, allowing sufficient time for some of our swollen bee stings to heal.

Here I should mention that bees frequently stung Trevor and me while on the road. At this point in the journey, by my estimation, I had been stung a number of times only comprehensible by those in the scientific field of astronomy. If all the tiny bee stingers that pierced my skin while riding had been collected and neatly laid end to end, they would have formed a line encircling the globe seven times.

"Seriously, how many times were you stung," you ask? Well, it's hard for me to nail down an exact number. I want to use the word *infinity*, but that's not really a number. Suffice it to say, many bees died defending some perceived attack of mine on their queen.

One incident stands out in my mind. The bee actually got into my helmet and became momentarily trapped between my sunglasses and my EYEBALL! As it buzzed furiously, no doubt fixated on my pupil like an archer on a bull's-eye, I remained calm and said a quiet prayer. No, wait; I screamed like a little girl and nearly lost control of the bike in an attempt to rip the glasses from my face. It stands out in my mind mostly because the bee did *not* sting me. When you think about it, it's really a wonder we managed to stave off the effects of anaphylactic shock.

Spending a few days in a hammock allowed the inflammation between me and Trevor to dissipate a little, too. We had kept up a unified front during the past several days, but all the stress and uncertainty of so many borders in so little time had taken its toll. We needed a little time to ourselves.

Through the trees in the courtyard, I could see Trevor sipping a Coke and writing in his journal. Occasionally we'd catch each other's eye from across the room, nod, lift our glasses and drink together, but we communicated little more than that during most of the day.

December 8

After leaving Granada, Trevor and I took a ferry to an island comprised of two majestic volcanoes and an isthmus located on Lago de Nicaragua. Approximately 100 kilometres of dirt road ring the Island of Ometepe in a misshapen figure eight.

It takes half a day to cross the island in extreme discomfort using the irregular bus service, but Trevor and I circumnavigated it in less than six hours. Since our bikes allowed access to the remotest parts of the island that buses cannot reach, we may actually have made first contact with some of the indigenous people… a theory supported by the stares we got as we bounced past them, waving and smiling like idiots.

We seldom shifted out of first or second gear, but we moved relatively fast. The spectacular scenery, as viewed through our visors, vibrated like a show on an old TV set with faulty vertical hold. No matter. With all its cavernous potholes, deep gashes and rocky protrusions, the road demanded our full attention.

A spreading tree beside an overgrown cemetery with whitewashed headstones offered respite for us and a troop of howler monkeys along a remote stretch of road. When we removed our helmets, the monkeys screamed at us and then retreated high into the canopy of our shady tree. As we watched them, a local family watched us. A muscular, dark-haired young man with a machete and a hint of suspicion in his eyes approached quietly from behind them. Before long, he invited us to follow him to his nearby shack where his family worked, packaging dry coffee beans in burlap sacks. With his permission, I snapped a few pictures of the man and his family. Meanwhile, Trevor ran around like a war photographer under fire, squatting here, dive-rolling there, in attempt to capture the perfect image.

We thanked the family for their time and returned to our machines. I had just strapped up my helmet when I noticed the man approaching us with a timid smile and a bunch of bananas. His smile broadened as he held out the bananas, but he remained silent. Trevor and I hesitated.

The thought of accepting a gift from this man, a gift given out of poverty, made me squirm. After all, I have little money by Canadian standards, but on a global scale I'm obscenely rich. And what if the roles were reversed? What if I found a grubby traveller parked outside of my house in Canada, would I invite him inside? Would I feed him or offer a gift?

A little twang of guilt reverberated in my heart when we took the bananas, but it served no purpose. The man had given to us what he could, and his warm smile reassured me that he was happy to do it. We ate the bananas together, right there on the road, before thanking him once more and finally bouncing away.

A decrepit brick *tienda* with a corrugated tin roof and earthen floor provided shade for our next rest stop. We sat at a plastic table beneath the only decoration in the dark shack – an advertisement featuring a scantily clad Britney Spears. I have to go with Tom Robbins on this one:

"The more advertising I see, the less I want to buy."

The old, one-eyed proprietor suppressed a look of shock when he saw us and hurried off to fetch warm sodas, smacking his young son on the back of the head as he left for staring at the strange white men.

December 11

Most people have to endure a two-hour hike to reach a picturesque waterfall on the small volcano, but walking is for suckers. After paying an entrance fee and riding through park gates, we motored through tall grass along a two-track path that veered to avoid pine trees and rock outcroppings as it climbed. Looking back, we could see the dark water of Lago de Nicaragua stretching to the horizon.

The trail rose sharply and twisted up increasingly difficult terrain, forcing us to stand on our foot pegs and lean heavily uphill. We rolled hard on the throttle in first gear, feathering the clutch to find a balance between momentum on the steep slope and control in the tight corners. The ride, at once exhausting and exhilarating, brought us to a rudimentary shelter on a sunlit, grassy bench. We parked the bikes and walked into a deep gorge filled with birdsong and broad-leaved plants.

A simple path, steep in spots and muddy, picked its way through the gorge over exposed roots along a peaceful stream. Where the clear water ran shallow and broad over smooth rock, we could skip across it on our toes in one or two quick strides. Where it flowed swift and narrow through a well-worn groove, we'd clear it in one little jump.

After about half an hour of hiking, we pushed through a curtain of waxy leaves into the cool air of a mossy amphitheatre that contained the falls. Nestled at the back of a tight, semicircular headwall, the water cascaded hundreds of feet down nearly vertical rock into a shallow pool lined with small round stones. No thundering torrent, these falls whispered politely so as not to interrupt the performance of an unseen avian symphony.

Trevor splashed around in the pool while I brooded over a growing problem – my intolerance towards Trevor. I'd lashed out at him in anger when we parked our motorbikes at the trailhead for the falls. In spite of the awkward manoeuvring required, Trevor insisted we padlock our bikes together with a thick cable we carry for that purpose. Given our remote location and the fact that we could easily lock the steering on our bikes, it seemed a complete waste of time and I exploded like a two-year-old who's just had a toy snatched away. My anger surprised us both and I sat at the falls trying to understand it.

Basically, it came down to efficiency. Whether intentionally or not, Trevor had been manipulating me and shaping our agenda simply by being slow. What had started out as my motorbike trip quickly became a joint venture that had quietly transformed into Trevor's itinerary. His pace dictated how far we rode each day, how long it took to find a hotel, how much time we had to explore our surroundings and, inevitably, how far south we could ride.

Once more I saw the ugly side of myself. I apologized to Trevor when he finished splashing around, and I meant it, but the resentment remained.

December 12

We arrived in Moyogalpa, on the island's coast, just in time to catch a ferry to the mainland. Large trucks stuffed with green bananas claimed most of the ferry's open deck. I quickly lashed my machine to a railing and clambered up the side of the ship to take pictures while Trevor battled ferry employees over how to stow his bike.

Once we got off the ferry a short ride brought us to San Juan del Sur, a small town on the Pacific Ocean near the border with Costa Rica, where we spent two days waiting for heavy rain to clear. I logged a lot of hammock time beneath the shelter of a clay tile roof, reading *Zen and the Art of Motorcycle Maintenance* and watching large turtles padding silently across the courtyard.

Trevor and I finally abandoned all hope of reaching South America. We made the decision based on time and money, but we had an unspoken understanding that our partnership could not endure the journey. We planned to explore the option of selling our bikes in Costa Rica and flying home. Failing that, we would have to drive the stupid things all the way back.

But, before getting rid of the bikes, we hoped to drive through Panama to the end of the road... the Darien Gap. There, we'd shout, "COLOMBIA SUCKS!" and drive away as fast as we could, giggling like schoolgirls. If all went to plan, the Colombians would never find us and we could be back in Canada before you could say "kidnapping."

December 15

Before leaving Canada, I carefully checked the travel advisories for every country between Mexico and Panama and they all said the same thing (I'm paraphrasing here): "Everybody stay home. If you are stupid enough to travel in Central America, you will be kidnapped, sodomized and killed, but not necessarily in that order. Certainly don't drive (you idiot), but if you must drive, keep your windows rolled up and doors locked at all times."

That last bit made me consider fitting my helmet visor with a padlock. But, so far, I had mostly good impressions of Central American people. They appeared friendly and honest (not counting the jerks that short-changed me at the gas stations in Mexico). They made travel in Central America a wholly pleasant experience... especially when compared to travel in, say, Egypt.

I visited the Middle East with a friend two months after terrorists destroyed the World Trade Center. Apparently, with my long blond hair and blue eyes, I represented a threat to Egyptian homeland security: the mere sight of me, obviously a "Western Christian," prompted several men in Cairo to shake angry fists at us and shout "OSAMA BIN LADEN!"

One day, Cordell and I witnessed a crowd beat a middle-aged woman into a bloody stupor. Another day, we saw a knife fight between three construction workers. (From that last scene I learned one important thing: never bring a shovel to a knife fight.)

In spite of that, we seldom felt physically threatened. However, virtually every shopkeeper, hotel manager and taxi driver we met in Egypt and then in Jordan swindled, cheated or deceived us in some way.

At first we presented easy targets, but we quickly became streetwise and belligerent. Unfortunately, Egyptians are highly adaptable. Watching them steal from us both infuriated and entertained us simultaneously.

At one point, Cordell and I passed a man selling mini-doughnuts from a little vending cart on the bank of the Nile River in Aswan. (Now, in several early drafts of this story I took an educated guess at the vendor's name, a name shared by more than half of all the Egyptian males we met during our travels. However, as the name bears religious connotations, my editor cautioned that such a reference might have an inflammatory effect upon certain individuals. In spite of my assurances that no one would ever actually read this book, she insisted I remove the name just to be on the safe side. Of course she's right. And so, to fully extinguish the flame of controversy, I must refer to the vendor as Dr. Mammary Ruttiger Von Straussenhammer III, Jr. I wouldn't want to be responsible for the sacking of any Canadian embassies.)

Anyway, Cordell and I needed doughnuts. Having learned a thing or two about the exorbitant prices Egyptians reserve for tourists, we first tried to see what price the locals paid. Mammary uncovered our plan rather quickly; neither Cordell nor I possesses subtlety as a strong mark of character.

He whispered something to his local patrons, who then cast sideways glances at us, concealing their money with their coats. Mammary took their money, made change under his little counter and, hiding it with his apron, gave it back to the customer. Mind you, these people worked as a team of swindlers with Mammary as their captain even though they had no vested interest in so doing.

Undaunted, Cordell and I approached the cart. Mammary pushed a bag of doughnuts at us and then wiped his hands on his greasy apron before fingering his thick moustache. In Egypt, if a merchant successfully places a product in your hands, he expects you to complete the transaction regardless of price. That tack didn't fly with us.

From experience we knew that the stated price would be ludicrous. Rather than bartering the price down, which could take as long as half an hour, Cordell often estimated the worth of a product, placed the money on the table and simply walked away. If the shopkeeper protested loudly and followed us to the door of his shop demanding more money, we'd paid more than we should have. If he protested by physically grabbing us and threatening to involve police, we'd paid the fair, local's price. If he followed us into the street, grabbed us and began calling for help, we needed to seriously reconsider our offer, but that only happened once.

Unfortunately, we didn't have exact change for the doughnuts. Cordell and I estimated the worth of a bag and handed Mammary some money, but he returned less than half the change we wanted.

"More," I insisted.

Mammary nodded in understanding and, feigning reluctance, placed two more doughnuts in the bag. Okay. That was funny.

"More MONEY," Cordell added in a confrontational tone, the only tone merchants understand.

The discussion became heated and Mammary finally obliged to give us more change. Originally, he had wanted five dollars. We paid 75 cents. Later, we learned that locals pay 20 cents. Such is daily life for a tourist in Egypt.

But, like I said, Central America had so far impressed us with the warmth of her people and we'd never felt physically threatened... until we entered Costa Rica – the safest of all Latin American countries, according to the *Lonely Planet*. To celebrate, we'd parked on a dirt pull-out in the shade of a Ceiba tree to enjoy a Bimbo. (It's not what you think. A Bimbo is just a Twinkie without the filling.) I was just about to say "And we rode here," when two police officers in a sputtering white truck approached us.

"Is everything all right?" the driver asked. We nodded.

"You shouldn't stay here," he said, almost conversationally. "It's very dangerous."

"What? Why?" I asked as he casually started driving away.

"Bandits!" exclaimed the enthusiastic passenger.

"Very dangerous," he added and playfully riddled me with bullets from an imaginary gun.

"They come out of the jungle from Nicaragua." He pointed to the dense, bandit-concealing greenery that pressed against our bikes.

"Thanks!" I yelled with a mouth full of Bimbo as I strapped up my helmet and started the engine. Trevor, usually eager to eat and hesitant to ride, was several steps ahead of me, but even he could not match the haste of our friendly police, who had already fled the scene in a cloud of dust.

That was our first taste of Costa Rica, dire warnings from friendly police. The next day we met some unfriendly police. First, I should provide a little background. In Central America, all signs displaying posted speed limits are purely decorative. If you ride 100 kilometres per hour in a 60 zone on an open highway, vehicles may slam into you from behind. Conversely, if you try riding the speed limit of 70 kilometres per hour on a precipitous mountain road, the mountain will shake you from its flanks like water from a wet dog. So you see, we had grown accustomed to ignoring speed limits by the time we reached Costa Rica.

Inevitably, some cops clocked Trevor going a little fast and pulled him over; I swear I saw dollar signs in their eyes when I pulled in behind him. They made various threats in choppy English, accompanied by throat-slicing motions to illustrate their point.

"You see?" asked the young cop (who bore a striking resemblance to Eric Estrada from *CHiPS*). He dragged his forefinger slowly across his throat. "Six months, no licence, no drive."

The old cop said nothing, but frowned and shook his head as if to say, "This is the part of the job I hate."

The cops both started writing tickets very, very slowly. They looked up to see if we understood the gravity of the situation. They continued writing.

"Or," the young cop said at last, pointing with his pen as if he'd just had an idea, "we could give you a warning."

"Yeah and how much does that cost?" I asked.

Trevor didn't wait for the reply. "That sounds good," he said. "We'll take the warning, then."

I carried two wallets for this very reason. One had all my money, identification and credit cards. The other had a few dollars and fake ID. I opened the wallet containing a few dollars.

"That's all we have," I lied. "We haven't been to the bank in Costa Rica yet."

Though disappointed, the police accepted our meagre offering and let us go.

Needless to say, for the rest of the ride to San José, we obeyed all posted speed limits.

We parked outside a quaint two-storey hostel in San José and went inside to get a room. When the kid at the front desk learned that we had left our bikes unattended, his jaw dropped and he fled the building as if it were on fire. We found him nervously pacing the sidewalk by our machines, imploring us to guard them against bandits. Perhaps certain travel advisories preach doom and gloom for good reason.

December 18

The high road from San José winds through a cloud forest. Now, in my mind, the term *cloud forest* conjures up images of cute, multi-coloured bears dancing on pillowy clouds and tending gardens of magical trees. The sobering reality: a forest perpetually enveloped in thick, cold fog and probably devoid of dancing bears.

I used the back of my hand to clear droplets of water from my visor, but still had trouble keeping Trevor's shadowy figure in sight through the mist. Soon my leather gloves were soaked and my fingers tingled with cold. As a remedy, I reached back to grasp my muffler. The muffler was located on the right side of the machine, so I had to really twist my body around to reach it with my left hand and, when grabbing it with my right, I had to cross over and hold the throttle with my left. No easy feat, but well worth the effort. It took only a minute for the hot metal of my exhaust pipe to completely dry out my gloves and warm my fingers.

Unfortunately, the trick did little to warm my body. When the shivering became uncontrollable, we stopped for a break at a lonely restaurant. A faded sign on the side of the building read, "Elevation 3,100 metres" (10,170 feet).

We sipped coffee by large picture windows overlooking the jungle canopy while dozens of shiny green and blue hummingbirds, ranging in size from peanuts to grapefruit, hovered at the feeders on the other side of the glass.

I thought about my grandma. She used to stand quite still by the hummingbird feeder in her back yard, holding out her finger like a perch. Occasionally, a bird would alight on her hand to access the feeder. She said it felt like an angel's kiss.

I saw her for the last time one month before she succumbed to liver cancer, lying on a couch and draped in a woollen blanket. If she'd had the energy to turn her head, she could have watched hummingbirds outside her living room window, but she could hardly move.

Still, even in her weakest moment, her face conveyed a peace that she quickly credited to faith in God. There, at death's door, gaunt, jaundiced and frail, she was beautiful and unafraid. While you may certainly debate the existence of God or whether faith in Jesus has merit, you cannot question the peace such faith gave my grandma. That, at least, was real.

It had been a long time since my last visit and when I entered the room I exclaimed, "Grandma, you look *fantastic!* Have you lost weight?" She managed a feeble laugh and then began to cough. She might have said the same thing if I were the one dying; her humour had always been a bit "edgy."

We had that in common, but I could identify with her for several other reasons. She loved travel and, having married late in life, she understood loneliness, too. She would have approved of this bike trip.

After a few short days I had to return to work in another province, knowing that the next time I saw my grandma she would be in a casket. I knelt beside the couch and leaned towards her, giving her a long, gentle hug. "Better make it good," she whispered. "This has to last a long time."

I told Trevor about my grandma and he listened quietly. When I finished we just sat there, silently watching the birds dart through the mist from one feeder to the next. To me, they represented the memory of a woman I admired for all of her love, courage, wisdom and strength. Suddenly they seemed like the most beautiful creatures in the world. I put my hand against the cold glass and a bird, no bigger than my thumb, paused for a moment just a few centimetres from my fingers, instantly replacing the cold in my body with a warm glow.

Trevor and I finished our coffee and left the restaurant. We prepared for another freezing ride, but the sun cracked the clouds as we descended, forcing us to stop and shed several layers of outer clothing.

Leaving the Pan-American Highway, we climbed towards San Vito along a narrow road that meandered in spots like Christmas ribbon candy. The road enjoyed a harmonious relationship with the landscape, as if it had merely intended to pass through but lay down for a rest on a carpet of thick grass and got lulled to sleep by whispering trees that stooped to offer it shade.

Gentle sunlight painted a canvas of verdant hills with millions of soft shadows, subtly accentuating every curve and dimple of the rolling terrain. Looking down, the Pacific Ocean sparkled like diamond dust, making the decision to stop for photos a no-brainer. I took a few shots of Trevor riding, and then we carried on our way.

Just when I thought the scenery had reached the earthly limitations of beauty, a single tree reminded me that beauty is boundless. It appeared in brilliant yellow bloom amidst a setting of deep, rolling green. Flowers shone from this tree where leaves should have been. We rode on and saw other bright yellow trees, but none was more striking than the very first.

After finding a hotel, we did some maintenance on our bikes. I adjusted the play in my throttle while Trevor took apart his entire rear brake assembly. With parts of his bike strewn about the sidewalk, it looked like he had ridden over a landmine. I wanted to capture the carnage on film, but I couldn't find my camera.

I had used it only a couple of hours ago, when I'd taken that photo of Trevor on the road. Had I been so pleased with myself for collecting the perfect image that I had winged the camera into the ditch in euphoric hysteria?

I had to find out. Trevor hurried to reassemble his bike, but I didn't have time to wait. Breaking our only rule, I rode, alone, into approaching darkness. The faint glow of my headlight reflecting off the pavement grew more and more pronounced as I raced to find the scene of our little photo shoot. A few traces of daylight remained when I reached the place, just enough to spot my camera lying beside the road. Apparently I had taken the shot, turned the camera off, placed it on the ground and driven away. Who does that?

Then again, I have a bit of a reputation when it comes to cameras. While volunteering at a wilderness camp one summer, the director asked me to lead a photography workshop for the sole reason that I owned an expensive camera. While I hurriedly packed my gear the night before the first day of the course, my precious camera fell off the top bunk and hit the bedroom floor with a disturbing thud. By all outward appearances it seemed all right, but when I tried to take a few test pictures the shutter refused to click open and the LED blinked as if it had a concussion.

I panicked. In desperation I phoned my dad, the only person I knew who had any technical knowledge of photographic equipment. Of course, he couldn't help me over the phone, but he offered to lend me his camera for the week. Within minutes of hanging up, he left his house in Saskatchewan and drove all night to meet me for breakfast.

"I'll take your camera back to Regina for repair," he offered. "Can I see it?"

He sat down and looked it over.

"See? The shutter won't click," I said.

"Hmm," he murmured, puzzling over the problem.

"And the LED is flashing."

He nodded. He could see that.

"Did you check the batteries?" he asked.

"Of course I checked the batteries." Did he think I was stupid?

"Why don't we put some film in it and see what happens?" he said.

"Film?"

"Yeah. There's no film in here."

Within eight hours and 30 seconds, my dad diagnosed the problem with my expensive camera: it had no film.

December 19

Our 11-year-old *tramitadore* guided us through the chaos of the Panamanian border in a record two hours. While waiting in line to clear customs, we met a father and son from Germany driving a green and black 1928 BMW around the world. They planned on a two-year journey and had a map of their travels painted on the side of their tiny car. We wished them luck before riding into Panama.

The air remained thick with humidity following an intense downpour as we pushed forward into dense jungle, a jungle whose dark hands seemed poised to strangle the slender road when no one was looking. We encountered more road construction. Just as we'd discovered in El Salvador, when workers close a lane for repair in Panama they simply put up a few pylons that force you into oncoming traffic. Roads and road rules in Latin America do not suffer fools.

We rented dirty, concrete rooms for the night in Tole, a town that barely warrants a dot on my map.

"We're in Panama," I said as I turned out the light. Trevor heard me from the next room.

"And we rode here," he responded quietly before falling asleep.

December 20

The grumpy old landlord came out to watch us pack in the morning. He wore the same sky-blue pants, white shirt with pockets and white woven hat from the night before. I pictured him in a large wicker chair, holding an ice tea, fanning himself and saying things like, "I can't divulge that information."

Following a slow ride on flat, straight roads, we reached the Bridge of the Americas spanning the Panama Canal. Crossing the bridge and rolling into Panama City, Trevor pumped his fist in the air, triggering our inaudible soundtrack, *Low Rider*; his left signal light served as a metronome for the music in my head.

With some difficulty, we found a room and then went in search of celebratory beer and cigars. Before we left the hotel, Trevor placed a phone call to some Colombian missionaries living in Panama City. I asked him how he knew them, but I didn't understand his answer; one of my least endearing traits of character is that I stop paying attention when someone uses more than one simple sentence to answer a question. Anyway, it didn't matter because the missionaries spoke no English and Trevor lost the connection a few seconds after they answered the phone. We took that as a sign from God that we should not contact these people, though Trevor did mention the name of our hotel just before getting cut off.

I had been eating a chocolate bar and waiting on the sidewalk while Trevor talked on the phone. The sun dropped out of sight, but I still wore sunglasses on my head. A young man in grubby clothes approached me, held out his hand and said succinctly in perfect English, "Hey man. Those are some nice shades. You're sitting there eating a Snickers bar, and it's Christmas." Unable to refute any of those statements, and clear of the implications, I handed him all the change in my pockets.

We found some nice cigars and took them to a nearby park to smoke.

A wildly drunken young man in a dirty white dress shirt sat beside us on the concrete bench. He eagerly welcomed us to his country and extended a filthy hand in friendship. Rather than shaking his hand I signalled with an enthusiastic thumbs-up, implying that such a greeting was customary amongst Canadians. I offered him the stub of my burning cigar. He mimicked the greeting and reluctantly accepted the stogie.

The man examined the smouldering gift tentatively from every angle before putting it timidly to his lips. Why he suddenly abandoned caution and drew on the stogie like he was trying to suck the water from a swimming pool I'll never know, but it triggered an ejaculation of saliva and mucus from nearly every observable orifice. The man embarked on a journey of convulsive hacking so violent that it may have deposited him momentarily on the doorstep of the spirit world, for after regaining his composure and sitting down, he stared at me with hollow eyes as if he had seen the face of God. In the ensuing moments of quiet reflection, the man may have thought of a question for God, because he slowly raised the cigar to his mouth and took another outrageously large hit with similar results, once more dancing recklessly on the thin line separating life and death.

Again he recovered and took his seat beside me, this time smiling and shaking his head as if he couldn't believe what had just happened. He politely offered me the cigar. When I refused to accept it, he extinguished it with his fingers and tucked it neatly in his shirt pocket, presumably in the event he ever wished to rephrase his question. With a wave and a nod, he stumbled to the ornamental fountain in the middle of the park, plunged his head into the stagnant water and came up with a mouthful, gargling.

We returned to the hotel to find two crazy Christians standing outside waiting for us – the Colombian missionaries. Apparently, they'd caught the name of our hotel just before getting cut off and decided to track us down.

Never have I met a man so perfectly fitting the description *roly-poly*. A chubby, short man, Einer had short black hair and light skin. He had a genuine smile that never left his face and a friendly energy that could transcend the mightiest barrier of language. He laughed easily and infectiously.

His wife, Girlesa, was also warm and friendly, though less animated than Einer, if only because it is impossible to be otherwise. She had beautiful dark skin and hair. She spoke a few words of English, but we mostly conversed in Spanish as a matter of necessity.

We talked for hours on the rooftop patio of a neighbouring hotel. Einer asked us to join him and a group of approximately 60 people headed for a mission's conference in Maje, a remote fishing village in the jungle. My default policy was still to refuse such invitations, despite the positive experience in Mexico with Peyore, but Trevor's eyes lit up like a kid in a candy store. A sense of dread washed over me.

I tried to bore a hole into Trevor's head with an intensely disapproving stare, but he ignored me. I watched in horror as Trevor copied detailed directions to Einer's house. I wanted to kick him under the glass table, but it was transparent and anyway the subtlety would be lost on Trevor. I just wanted to go to bed and carry on the next day as though I had never met these people. I didn't want to step *that far* out of my comfort zone. Was I not uncomfortable enough already? Apparently not.

December 21

Just before sunset, Trevor and I locked our motorbikes inside a small, empty room adjoining Einer and Girlesa's apartment and caught a bus with them to a river port outside of town where we waited.

We waited for hours.

Under a black and moonless sky on an unholy dock that reeked of rotten fish, human waste and other pungent but unidentifiable smells, with 60 people we did not know, we waited. Somewhere on the dark river deep in the Panamanian jungle, four boats laboured upstream to meet us and take us into the night to an unknown destination. Originally, Einer had talked Trevor into a 45-minute boat ride in the light of day. The ride, when it finally came around midnight, would last for 14 hours.

I had a bad feeling.

I thought about my bike, abandoned and vulnerable with only Trevor's machine to keep it company in a concrete room far from home. I had never left it alone for more than a few hours on this trip so far. Was it really secure? Would it still be there when I got back?

After all, according to popular opinion, most movies I've seen and books I've read, religious leaders have ulterior motives. Einer didn't appear to advocate genocide, pedophilia or cultural oppression, but he was a missionary; perhaps he operated a chop shop and our machines had already been dismantled and sold for parts on the black market.

As the worst-case scenarios reached alarming proportions in my imagination, I became furious with Trevor for placing our trip at risk. Had it been up to me, I would have avoided the entire situation. I hardly spoke to him all day, but brooded silently, occasionally shooting Trevor an angry glance to make sure he didn't enjoy himself too much.

But, as stars blinked on one by one in the sky over the filthy dock and we continued to wait, I thought about the absurdity of our situation, and it forced me to smile. To put things in perspective, I did a short review: after riding my motorbike all the way from Canada, I had locked it in a vacant apartment in Panama City to catch a midnight boat destined for a remote village in the jungle, at Christmas. I had wanted an adventure, hadn't I?

And, as for Einer, with every passing moment I grew to like him more. His love for people became evident as he wandered through the crowd, speaking and laughing with nearly everyone. From time to time he stepped aside to check on Trevor and me, calming my nerves with a kindness that felt sincere and free. I came to trust him. It occurred to me that the bad apples of any group get all the press.

When our boat finally arrived, we waded into murky water, threw our bags in the bow and climbed over the side. Passengers crowded together on the high wooden benches like swallows in the rafters of a barn. With limited seating, many passengers stood on the wet deck, leaning on gunwales for support. Each of the four boats carried some 20 people plus cargo.

Trevor and I had nothing to complain about. Einer provided us with seats of honour in the bow, stretched out on all the packs. Then, as if to underscore the gap between socio-economic classes, I had the audacity to inflate my Therm-a-Rest and construct the most comfortable seat you can imagine. We turned downstream and I dozed restlessly to the drone of an underpowered outboard motor.

I awoke in the dead of night on the open ocean, miles from shore.

The churning water in our wake shone with phosphorescence from some sort of algae that reminded me of fireflies on a summer night in southern Manitoba. The water glowed so vigorously that when I reached over the gunwale to touch it, my arm cast a shadow on the side of the boat.

The night passed slowly. A dolphin played near our bow in the grey light of early morning and, in a flash, the sun peeked over the jungle.

With no shade on the open water, the temperature rose sharply and we kept motoring. I wandered in and out of consciousness, under a merciless sun, with the sort of restless but heavy sleep that comes with heat and dehydration. Every time I awoke I had to force my eyelids open. My head throbbed and my swollen tongue felt like it had gained 15 pounds overnight.

We left the ocean and turned up another stream to find ourselves back in the steamy jungle. The heavily-laden boats kept running aground in the shallow water of low tide, forcing us to wade ashore and beat our way through thick vegetation along the swampy riverbank to our final destination – a fishing village with dozens of thatched-roof shacks on stilts.

We stumbled out of the jungle, covered in mud, drenched with sweat, and dotted with bug bites. From the time we'd left the city to the time we dropped our packs on the rough-hewn timber floor of our Christmas home, 24 hours had elapsed. The village remained blissfully archaic except for a solitary satellite telephone booth and, more importantly, a propane-powered fridge belonging to our host family and stocked with cold Pepsi.

I closed my eyes and cradled the cold bottle, beaded with condensation, against my cheek. I opened it. "*Hissssss,*" it said.

"What?" I whispered to the effervescent fluid dancing in the bottle, now held to my ear.

"You want me to drink you?" I asked. "But, I love you." I held the bottle to my ear again. Little bubbles leapt from its open mouth and tickled my face.

"AHHAHAH!" I exclaimed as everyone turned to watch me. "Okay. Okay. I'll drink you, my little sugar-saturated container of love."

I believe I may have kissed the bottle at that point. The sweet nectar stung my parched lips and tongue, burning my throat with every euphoric swallow.

December 24

The locals were descended from the Wounaan Indians, indigenous to the Darien jungle. Their language required strange inflection, often holding high-pitched syllables for seconds before finishing a word or sentence. When they spoke, it sounded like singing.

After a breakfast of fish, rice, plantains and unidentifiable rubbery creatures that may have fallen into the cauldron by accident, we paddled a flat-bottomed boat with several youths up a languid stream to a kind of aquatic hunting ground. Armed with metal spears, we dove into clear pools for freshwater shrimp.

The spears were only about two feet long. They had a length of rubber surgical tubing attached to one end with a small loop for your thumb. You drew the spear across the back of your hand like an arrow in an invisible bow. When released, the arrow cut through the water with startling speed, leaving a contrail of bubbles to mark its trajectory. It was a simple, highly effective design.

The boys made it look easy. Floating through the pool, creating barely a ripple, they carefully scanned the river bottom for prey through their diving masks. They moved slowly against the gentle current until they spotted a target. Regulating their buoyancy through careful breathing, they exhaled to slip silently beneath the surface with the deadly stealth of a hunting crocodile. They almost always surfaced with a writhing creature on the end of their spears.

As for me, my technique never had the hallmark of finesse. I muddied the water, kicking up a cloud of silt from the streambed and, when unexpectedly confronted by a trio of large fish, I screamed. I screamed underwater. It sounded remarkably like the cry of a child who, joyfully blowing bubbles in his chocolate milk, gets snuck up on from behind and startled by a mischievous guardian. (I know. I've since verified that fact while babysitting my friend's two-year-old son.)

Once I regained my composure, I managed to locate a shrimp that had backed itself into a little hollow, leaving no escape. Well, I didn't find it exactly. One of the boys, following a quick assessment of my hunting savvy, corralled the critter and called me over to make the kill.

Together, the boy and I sank to the bottom of the pool, where he directed me to my prey. Leaving nothing to chance, I slowly drew near until the quivering tip of my drawn spear came to rest about two centimetres from the shrimp. The beast recoiled slightly in fear. Then I let fly, scoring a perfect hit and screaming underwater once again, this time in delight. I had submerged as a hunting neophyte, but surfaced a hunter... a mighty hunter. I had killed food.

Then Trevor took his turn. If my style could be described as humorously clumsy, then Trevor's could only be described as pure comedy. Upon target acquisition, he'd take an enormous breath and hold it in anticipation of a mighty submarine struggle. Of course, with his lungs full of air he floated like a rubber duck. Then he'd stick his bum in the air as if he could breathe through it and splash like a toddler in a piddle pool. When he couldn't hold his breath any longer, he'd exhale, momentarily submerge, and then struggle back to the surface, gasping for air. This pattern was repeated until all wildlife within a half-mile radius had escaped to a more tranquil location.

That evening, Trevor and I reluctantly partook of our bounty. The boys presented us with a steaming bowl of boiled shrimp, mostly a product of their efforts, I might add, and we slowly picked away at them, eating the entire bowl over the course of the night.

December 25

In the absence of gaudy decorations, rampant commercialism and stop-animation TV shows starring Burl Ives, I could hardly believe it was Christmas. Further adding to my disbelief, the clothing on my sweat-soaked body clung to me like Saran Wrap on a Jell-O salad.

In spite of the heat and humidity that made every movement painfully difficult, we spent the day wandering the village with a gaggle of children who eagerly lined up to watch their friends through the telephoto lens on Trevor's camera. Later, I found a perfect black tarantula on a path. I toyed with the idea of capturing it until Trevor pointed out that it would be difficult to organize a helicopter evacuation.

December 26

The conference ended and it was time to return to civilization. In order for the boats to navigate the shallow stream, we left well before dawn to coordinate our departure with high tide. Our breakfast consisted of smoked fish and plain rice wrapped in aluminum foil.

Ten hours after leaving the village, Trevor and I burst through the door of Einer and Girlesa's house in Panama City to check on our motorcycles. Finding them safe and soundly locked, we uttered soft, affectionate words of greeting, touching the bikes tenderly and finally climbing onto the seats with heavy sighs of relief.

When I'd left Canada, I had promised God and myself that I would not fall in love with my motorbike. I would treat it without passion as a machine, a tool that made possible a certain objective. But the bike became a team member. More than that, it became my friend.

I ran my fingers over the sun-bleached plastic fender and picked at a sticker of a Canadian flag that had turned completely white. Beneath the sticker, the fender remained dark green, like the jungles of Panama. Spots of rust grew in the scratches on the silver gas tank, and the bark busters proudly displayed fractures like medals for bravery. As the bike got uglier it became more endearing to me. How could I possibly sell it in Costa Rica?

Trevor and I looked a little the worse for wear ourselves. Later that day, as I sat on my motorbike mending a large tear in the seat of my white denim shorts with strawberry-flavoured dental floss, I began to see just how haggard we looked. Trevor's red Coca-Cola shirt had turned pink from the sun, and his thin plaid work shirt had become tattered and translucent. Watching him repair little tears in its fabric made me think of a man sewing together sheets of toilet paper. My favourite T-shirt had faded, stretched and grown threadbare at the shoulders, tearing apart at the seams. When I gently tried to remove the sleeves, the shirt ripped in two.

I thought about the journey home, fearing that, like the shirt, my partnership with Trevor would fall apart under the strain. We would rest for a few days with Einer in Panama, but it was definitely time to go home.

December 27

We took a bus to Casco Antiguo, an old part of Panama City built on a peninsula jutting into the Pacific. The peninsula overlooked the modern skyline of Panama City to the east, and the Panama Canal and Bridge of the Americas to the west.

Streaked with obsolete rail lines, brick streets adorned the feet of colourful colonial buildings in Casco Antiguo. Balconies displayed iron railings and red flowers, while dilapidated buildings packed with impoverished tenants hid behind the idyllic façade. Helpful police spent their days whisking ignorant tourists, like us, from the unsightly slums, plopping them safely back on the shiny tourist path.

We walked along the oceanfront on an elevated promenade and watched large tankers queuing for the canal. Leaving the walkway, we ducked into an air-conditioned café to avoid a sudden, ferocious rain and order coffee.

For the first time in days, Trevor and I had an actual conversation rather than an argument. Because of his back problems, Trevor still wanted to sell his machine in Costa Rica and fly home. I had tentatively decided to ride home, but enduring all those kilometres and crossing all those borders without Trevor seemed like a daunting task. Besides, we had started out as a team and we both agreed that we'd like to finish as one. I didn't know what to do.

December 28

Trevor and I took a bus to the Miraflores Locks on the Panama Canal. As we walked across the parking lot we noticed a 2002 Kawasaki KLR 650 registered in Alberta. It sat low to the ground. Most of the bike's milky green plastic lay hidden beneath a patchwork of stickers and duct tape. A rusty iron grate, welded to the frame, protected the radiator and gave the bike a utilitarian look. The luggage rack consisted of ill-fitting steel tubing and chromed pieces of luggage systems scavenged from other bikes and held together by a colourful web of bungee cords.

I checked the odometer. It had 33,500 kilometres, which encouraged me as mine only had 24,700. We were leaving a note on the bike when its owner returned. We introduced ourselves.

"Yeah, I wondered when I was going to run into you guys," said Mike as though it were a foregone conclusion. "I heard about you two in Nicaragua and I've been trying catch you ever since."

Mike had stayed at the Bearded Monkey in Granada and the owners had mentioned us. Since then, he had heard intermittent rumours of two Canadians travelling by motorcycle at nearly every town he visited.

"So, what possessed you two to do this trip?"

"I'm running away from a girl," said Trevor, sort of jokingly, but not really.

"Yeah, me too," said Mike.

"Well, I guess we're all here because of a girl," I laughed.

"Oh, every biker is," said Mike emphatically, then, a little slower and quieter, as if to himself, "every biker is."

Together, we watched a ship pass through the locks. Mike tried various methods of persuasion, to most of which I've been immune since junior high, to convince Trevor and me to ship our bikes into Colombia and continue riding to Argentina with him. I actually thought about it, but once the decision to go home has been made it's tough to consider other options. Mike's enthusiasm accomplished one thing, though; I made up my mind, right then and there, that I would ride home. I didn't tell Trevor.

December 29

As we packed our bikes to leave, Einer gave us most of his earthly possessions. In spite of our objections, he insisted we each accept a small wooden carving of an osprey from the village we had visited. The smooth brown carvings were about six centimetres tall; each bird perched atop a square-based dome with its head cocked to the left. Mine remains one of my most precious possessions and represents some of my favourite memories. To think, I never would have experienced the jungle adventure if not for Trevor.

After waving goodbye, Trevor popped a little wheelie and roared through the gates of the compound, to everyone's delight. Not to be outdone, and taking no time to think or prepare, I revved my engine to 5,000 rpm and dumped the clutch from a standing start, sending my front wheel rocketing into the air. Rather than instinctively applying the rear brake to lower my front end, I instinctively splayed my legs out to the side in some misguided hope that such action could avert catastrophe. How my instincts routinely fail me — and I remain alive — is the reason I'm a creationist.

I didn't crash and, when my front wheel slammed back to earth, I waved to everyone like I meant to do that and rode away very, very slowly. Trevor led us out of the city. For the first time in months, we pointed our machines towards home and rode confidently on familiar roads.

Afterword

For New Year's Eve we took shelter from a cold rain in Boquete, a village in the Panamanian highlands near Volcán Barú. Between swigs of horrible Panamanian beer, and concussive explosions from unreasonably powerful bottle rockets, Trevor told me that he would like to ride back to Canada. I suppressed a smile and breathed a quiet sigh of relief; we had been getting along much better since our jungle excursion, but we still opposed each other's ideas by default and I feared Trevor might change his mind if he knew that I wanted him to ride home with me.

Riding north, border crossings took half the time they had on the way south due in part to our relaxed attitudes towards *tramitadores* and bribery. We breezed into Costa Rica, staying at a familiar hostel in San José and depositing our bikes at a Kawasaki dealer for service. In addition to checking our valves and installing a new drive tire on my bike, the dealer washed our machines and glazed every surface with a shiny, slippery polish, including the brake rotors. Of course, slippery brake rotors may well serve as a powerful illustration in any debate on form versus function, and we nearly slammed into the back of several vehicles on the ride out of San José before the polish burned off.

We hurried into Nicaragua to meet Trevor's parents, who happened to be serving as volunteers with a humanitarian project in the country. Mr. and Mrs. Martens put us up in their spacious hotel room in Granada, which featured hot water, a toilet with a toilet seat, and an air conditioner capable of blanketing the room in a thin layer of frost.

Approaching the Honduran border, we carefully followed our maps, which contradicted each other and led us horribly off-route, along a

107

road of interlocking driveway bricks, into hills dotted with large pine trees. When we found the border, Honduran officials cheated us out of an indeterminate amount of money and threatened to deny us access to their country when Trevor stubbornly objected.

We crossed the border and rode north to the island of Utila, where we spent a week scuba diving before turning towards the Mayan ruins of Copán, near the Guatemalan border. We crossed into Guatemala without *tramitadores* or bribes in less than an hour and quickly found the main highway to Guatemala City. We bypassed the capital on miles of gravel roads, riding towards Amatitlán for the night. Unable to find suitable accommodations, we continued south in the twilight towards Palin, where the sun finally set on our unsuccessful search. Circumstances forced us to ride in the dark towards Esquintla, a city described in my *Lonely Planet* guidebook thusly: "Surrounded by rich, green foliage, Esquintla should be a relaxed tropical idyll. But it's actually a hot, dingy, dilapidated industrial city that's... (not) important to travelers."

We read the discouraging description by the faint bluish glow of my LED headlamp at the outskirts of the city. A friendly shirtless man with a cocked pistol stuffed in his pants approached and directed us to an auto hotel, which means "sexual playground" in Guatemala. No idea seems good when it's coming from a man with a loaded gun in his pants, but we had no choice. We reluctantly paid an attendant – who kept winking at us knowingly as we checked in – an hourly rate for a brazen red room with ceiling mirrors. At least we had air conditioning and TV; a TV that turned on mysteriously at three in the morning to Supertramp's bouncy and disturbingly appropriate hit, *Take the Long Way Home*.

After spending less than 48 hours in Guatemala, we arrived at the Mexican frontier at Tapachula and bumped into the very first *tramitadore* we'd ever hired. We chatted for a while, but he offered no help – he could see we didn't need any.

We raced to the east coast of Mexico like a couple of horses catching sight of the barn. The temperature became noticeably cooler as we neared the US border, and I e-mailed my dad, letting him know that we were on schedule. Before I'd set out on this trip, I had asked him if he would be willing to drive as far as Texas to pick me up with his truck; I wanted to avoid riding into a Canadian winter. He never hesitated. "Yeah. I can do that." He dropped everything at work and drove south to meet us.

Of course, the only time in four months that we needed to be at a certain place at a certain time I developed mechanical problems: my shift lever snapped just as we rolled into Tampico for night.

The next morning we encountered an old man in a tiny hardware store who drew us a map to a welder. The welder lived above his shop and might be able to help us, even on a Sunday. We found the welder washing his car. He dropped what he was doing and fixed the lever in 15 minutes. We never even had time to panic. (Well, Trevor didn't; I can always find time to panic.)

As we rode to San Fernando, I battled that familiar depression that creeps up near the end of every chapter of life. The next day would see us Stateside.

It was January 27, 2004; four months and 15,000 kilometres had passed since I'd left Canmore. The day started out cold and got colder the farther north we rode. As if to make the most of our final opportunity to screw up, we blew past the Mexican border and nearly crossed the toll bridge into the States without clearing our paperwork. We turned around, rode the wrong way up one-way access roads and reported to Mexican customs.

Following a shockingly incomplete search on the US side, we rode into Texas.

"WE'RE IN THE STATES!" Trevor yelled as we rode away from the border.

"AND WE RODE HERE!" I shouted.

In the US such a proclamation seemed pathetically anti-climactic, but we were nothing if not consistent, and pathetic. When we pulled into a rest stop along the Texas highway for a break from the cold, a trucker noticed our bikes and came over to talk to us.

"Where y'all headed?" he asked.

"Canada," Trevor replied.

"You guys are crazy. Where y'all been?"

"We drove all the way to Panama City, actually."

"Panama City. So that's in Texas?"

"No. It's in Panama... the country."

"Panama? Where's that?"

"It's south and a little east of Mexico, Guatemala, El Salvador, Honduras, Nicaragua and Costa Rica."

"No shit!"

"No shit."

"Y'all are crazy." He walked away shaking his head. We shook our heads as he walked away, too.

We pitched our tent in the back yard of a little church in Corpus Christi – more missionary contacts of Trevor's. I settled into my sleeping bag and tried not to think about the cold. It was the last uncomfortable night that Trevor and I would spend together. Our friendship, which was fragile from the start, had all but evaporated. After spending so much time together under stress, we had nothing more to say to one another, even though we had shared so much.

My dad had ridden his motorcycle with me in the beginning, and he was with me in the end. He gave the trip symmetry. Trevor and I hardly spoke to each other on the drive home, and when my dad and I dropped him off in Manitoba the farewell was decidedly unemotional.

Trevor and I went our separate ways and immediately lost touch with each other; it seemed to be a mutual decision and I didn't miss him.

In the months that followed, I opened up my trip journal to see if I'd accomplished anything in the four months on the road. I had undertaken the journey to breathe life into a hollow heart. The edge had come off my loneliness, but that could be attributed to time. I still felt a little numb, not because I missed Susan, but because I missed the piece of me that had died with our relationship. Perhaps I would never be the same. So what had I accomplished? I'd left with a hollow heart and returned with a hollow heart and a nasty list of character flaws. I'd taken a weak friendship and destroyed it.

The carving Einer gave me sat on my desk, glaring at me with angry wooden eyes. Its perfection reminded me of my flaws: flaws that I've always had, flaws that I may rage against but never change. Still, I reasoned, as any therapist will tell you, recognizing a problem is the first step towards correcting it. What had I accomplished? I could see a little better who I was, and who I wanted to be.

A year went by before the lines of communication re-opened between Trevor and me with an e-mail that simply read, "Hey. Are you still alive?" The reply: "Yeah. Do you still have your bike?" Intermittent e-mails and phone calls ensued and, 18 months after I'd dropped him in Manitoba, Trevor rode his KLR, laden with gear, to Canmore on his way to the west coast.

Seeing him pull into my driveway almost made me cry. I felt ashamed of how we'd parted ways and eager to make amends. Could Trevor forgive me? He got off the bike and we exchanged one of those awkward handshakes that turn into a manly hug with lots of backslapping. The next day I loaded some basic gear onto my bike and we rode south into the mountains.

Wispy clouds, getting snagged and torn on jagged limestone peaks, bled rain onto the talus and dark fir trees. Puddles gathered in every depression of the muddy road. The green of our bikes appeared almost obscene, the only flash of colour in a moody landscape of black and white. What a contrast to the warm, green mountains of Central America, where everything around us had colour and the storms remained mostly internal.

On this day, the damp and the cold failed to darken our spirits. Splashing through puddles afforded photo opportunities. Throwing rooster-tails of wet gravel with our back wheels provided entertainment. Soaked to the bone, we spoke affectionately of the miserable riding conditions at every stop.

Some time over the past year and a half, Trevor had learned to cancel his left signal light. Other than that, it felt just like we were back on the same trip, only we got along. We quickly fell into old patterns. We could tell when the other rider wanted to stop for a break or a photo; it just all clicked.

We stopped for the night in Fernie, BC, our bikes and gear covered with mud after riding in the rain all day. Over supper that night we talked about memories from the trip, and the next trip we would like to do.

The next morning we loaded up in the rain. We rode west along Highway 3 to Cranbrook, stopping at the junction with Highway 93 where we would go our separate ways, Trevor to the coast and me back to Canmore. Once again, we hardly spoke. Only this time, it was not because we were tired of one another, but because we had said every necessary thing. Maybe we would never ride together again. Maybe there would not be another long trip. But, the point is, there could be.

We embraced again, this time finding it quite easy. I said goodbye and strapped up my helmet. "Now the trip is over," I thought. "I can feel good about ending this way." I was just about to ride off when Trevor snuck up behind me and punched me in the back of the head. I watched him run away in my mirror as the rain trickled down my back. "Okay. *Now* the trip is over."

Acknowledgements

Thanks to the "Enigmatic Tradesman" for showing me that logic is merely a chalice we use to drink from the River of Truth, whatever that means. Thanks to Valerie Bechtold for helping me transform a long, poor manuscript into a short, mediocre one and to Corinne Webb for helping me write even gooder. My editor, Yvonne Jeffery, offered many helpful insights, taking a bunch of stuff and finding a story. Matt Jackson, author of *The Canada Chronicles*, provided mentorship and loads of assistance.

To Trevor Martens, thank you for not launching a libel suit. To Trevor's new bride, God help you. Jae'than Reichel forced me to continue when I wanted to quit and Jeff Renaud convinced me that "The *Real* Diary of Anne Frank" was an inappropriate title. Also, the following people: Deborah Lantz, Tom Wolfe, and Lynda and Leighton Poidevin, advised against the following titles: "Seven Pillars of Gypsum," "Bum Sauce" and "Wide World of Fish." Chris Becker keeps telling me that he contributed in some way and demanding that his name appear in the acknowledgements. Scott from Scott Manktelow Design created the cover and maps, demonstrating remarkable patience with me – "Now can we delete all those towns I forced you to find?" Jennifer Groundwater put some final touches on the book and provided great feedback. Special thanks to Chris Scott and Grant Johnson for taking time to read the manuscript and offer suggestions. Thanks to the Zygorthian Chronicles; true, you didn't provide any actual support or help me in any way, but you didn't try to stop me, either.

To Stuart Kroeker, we'll always have Nintendo. And finally, thanks to my parents – uh, without you, I wouldn't exist.

About the Author

First and foremost, **Jeremy Kroeker** is a culinary idiot. Born in 1973 in the Mennonite Mecca of Steinbach, Manitoba, he immigrated to the Canadian Rockies and Canmore, Alberta where he discovered that certainty of knowledge is guarded by a hedge of insanity. But, mostly he just eats a lot of canned soup.

For contact information and additional therapy, visit
www.jeremykroeker.com

ISBN 141207832-6

9 781412 078320